The architecture of
Stations and Terminals

D1515278

Stations and Terminals

AUTHOR
Francisco Asensio Cerver

EDITORIAL MANAGER
Paco Asensio

PROJECT COORDINATOR
Ivan Bercedo (Architect)

TEXT

Michael Webb

DESIGN AND LAYOUT
Mireia Casanovas Soley

PHOTOGRAPHERS

Timothy Hursley, Nick Merrick (Denver Airport); Alex Levy (Lille Airport); Paul Maurer (Terminal B of Bordeaux Airport); Paul Maurer (Pointe à Pitre Airport); Jannes Linders, Claes de Vrieselaan (West terminal and Plaza at Schiphol); Klaus Frahm, Heiner Leiska, G. Grimmenstein (Hamburg Airport); Andrew Ward, Richard Davies (Stansted Airport); Richard Bryant/Arcaid (Stuttgart Airport); Ralph Richter/Architekturphoto (TGV Station at the Airport of Lyon-Satôlas); Paul Maurer (Charles de Gaulle Airport Interchange Module); Jiri Havran (Slependen Station); Jiri Havran (Sandvika Station); Richard Barnes (The Solana Beach Transit Station); David Manchón, Joanjo Rios (Sabadell Station); Accent Visuel, Stéphane Spack, Rob Fleck, L. Lecat (Tram Station in Strasbourg); Lluís Sans (Bilbao Subway); Paolo Rosselli (Alameda Bridge Subway Station); George Fessy (Vénissieux Parilly Subway Station); O.H.Fency (Place de L'Homme de Fer); Thomas Deutschmann (Bus Stops)

First published in 1997 by Arco for
Hearst Books International
1350 Avenue of the Americas
New York, NY 10019

Distributed in the U.S. and Canada by
Watson-Guptill Publications
1515 Broadway
New York, NY 10036

Distributed throughout the rest of the world by
Hearst Books International
1350 Avenue of the Americas
New York, NY 10019

1997 © FRANCISCO ASENSIO CERVER

ISBN: 0-8230-0257-8

PRINTED IN SPAIN

No part of this publications may be reproduced,
stored in retrieval system or transmitted in any form or by means,
electronic, mechanical, photocopying, recording or otherwhise, without
the prior written permission of the owner of the copyright.

Airports

THE WORLD'S GREAT CAPITALS, SUCH AS TOKYO, NEW YORK, FRANKFURT, AND MEXICO CITY, ALL HAVE THEIR OWN ARCHITECTURAL TRADITIONS SET AGAINST A UNIQUE CULTURAL BACKGROUND. AT THE SAME TIME, HOWEVER, THESE DIVERSE CITIES HAVE AT LEAST ONE SURPRISING ELEMENT IN COMMON: THEIR AIRPORTS.

AIRPORTS SERVE AS A KIND OF INTERNAL BORDER OR FRONTIER BETWEEN A NATION AND THE REST OF THE WORLD. THE BOUNDARY IS NEARLY AS STRIKING AND PALPABLE AS ANY OTHER, ALTHOUGH IT IS IMPOSSIBLE TO TRACE ON ANY MAP. HOWEVER, THIS IS A BORDERLAND IN FLUX. DURING THE PAST DECADE, ARCHITECTS AND THE PUBLIC HAVE GROWN IMPATIENT WITH THE STERILE, UNREMARKABLE DESIGNS THAT WERE FOR SO LONG THE HALLMARK OF AIRPORT BUILDINGS.

PERHAPS BECAUSE OF THE DAUNTING COMPLEXITY OF MANAGING URBANIZATION, OR PERHAPS BECAUSE OF THE SEDUCTION THAT SUCH COMPLEXITY PROVOKES IN ARCHITECTS, A COMPELLING IDEA IS EMERGING, THE IDEA OF BUILDING AS CITY—THE NOTION OF A BUILDING WITH ITS OWN INTERNAL COMMUNICATIONS, LIVING SPACES, AND FACILITIES FOR BUSINESS AND RELAXATION. THESE META-BUILDINGS ARE CITIES, BUILT AT A SCALE THAT CAN BE MANAGED.

THIS IS NOT NECESSARILY A NEW IDEA. WE SEE IT ALSO IN FOURIER AND IN LE CORBUSIER. IN CONTRAST TO THOSE EARLIER THINKERS, HOWEVER, ARCHITECTS MAY NO LONGER BE CONCERNED SOLELY BY DEMANDS ASSOCIATED WITH SOCIAL INTERACTIONS. THEY ALSO FACE THE SHEER CHALLENGE OF COPING WITH THE ENORMOUS MOVEMENT OF GOODS AND PEOPLE MADE POSSIBLE BY TODAY'S TRANSPORTATION SYSTEMS. AIRPORTS, FOR EXAMPLE, MUST BE VIEWED MORE AS URBAN CENTERS THAN AS MERE NEXUS POINTS IN A GRID.

AN AIRPORT AT THE EDGE OF A METROPOLITAN AREA MUST ACCOMMODATE A STEADY TORRENT OF TRAVELERS, WHO OFTEN CONNECT WITH THE AIRPORT FROM OTHER TRANSPORTATION NETWORKS, AND WHO REQUIRE A FULL RANGE OF SERVICES. RETAIL SHOPS, HOTELS, LEISURE ACTIVITY CENTERS, FINANCIAL CENTERS, AND SO ON, MUST NOW SPRING UP IN THE DIRECT SHADOW OF THE AIRPORT. AS A RESULT, AIRPORTS ARE NO LONGER SIMPLY GATEWAYS TO A CITY, BUT RATHER THE TERRITORY OF HIGH-SPEED NOMADS.

Denver Airport

DENVER, COLORADO, 1994

Airports often have more in common with each other than with the cities they are meant to serve. Out of obvious necessity, airports must be located on the flattest, most featureless, and most isolated stretches of land available. Worse still, the buildings themselves often seem excessively utilitarian and bleak, as though intended to be transited only for a brief and thoughtless moment.

Federico Peña, Denver's mayor at the time, had a different idea for the new airport. He wanted it to be a proud and memorable symbol of the city. Denver is a hub airport for routes on many airlines. For that reason, the airport is visited by millions of travelers whose final destination is not necessarily Denver itself. Having a distinctive airport to make a lasting and positive impression, therefore, was an especially important concern.

Even in Fentress' very first rough sketches for the terminal, we can clearly recognize the jagged, sinuous lines that distinguish it today. Geographically, Denver lies along the "front range." This is the line at which the seemingly endless flat expanse of the North American prairie is suddenly punctuated by the jagged edge of the Rocky Mountains. Fentress' design seeks to capture the movement and drama of this geography, and in so doing, to make a lasting impression on air travelers.

Images showing differing impressions given by the terminal, depending on distance and time of day.

Early sketch of the airport showing Fentress's initial conceptualization.

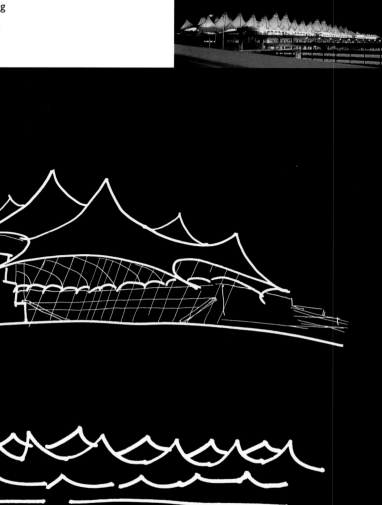

The terminal is laid out symmetrically along its transverse axis. The layout is quite simple, consisting of an elongated central building with a large, multilevel central lobby, with each level dedicated to a specific function. On both sides of the central building are three blocks, each having several floors of parking space. The central lobby is covered with an enormous sheet of canvas supported on two rows of pillars and stretched taut. Two roads carry traffic to the upper level. One end of the transverse axis of the building connects with other airport installations, such as a hotel, offices, and the control tower. At the other end, the terminal can readily be expanded in the future by using the same block-like scheme.

The terminal at dusk. The canopy is not opaque, and in fact allows some light to pass into the terminal during the day and out of it at night.

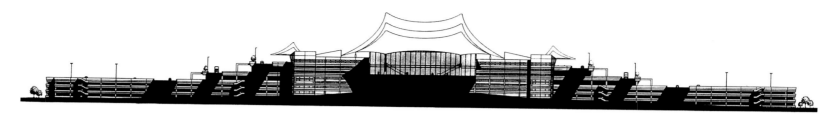

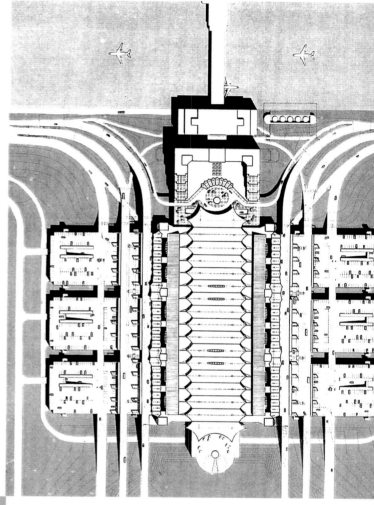

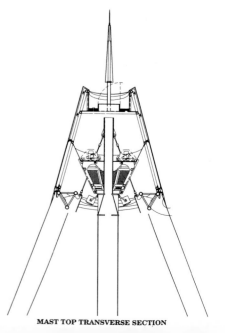

MAST TOP TRANSVERSE SECTION

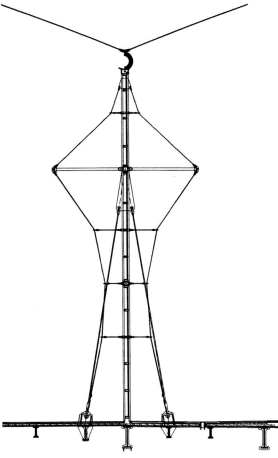

SOUTH WALL CABLE TRUSS SECTION

From the simplest camping tent to the surprising shapes created by Frei Otto for the Olympic Village in Munich: the use of durable membranes drawn taut by cables is perhaps one of humanity's oldest technologies, and ironically one of its subtlest and most complex technologies, as well.

United/United Express

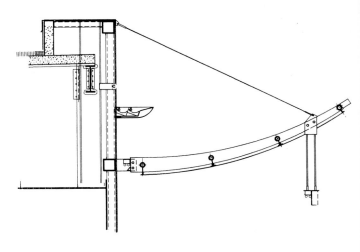

TICKET COUNTER CANOPY

13

Several views of the central lobby. The columns supporting the canopy roof are similar in shape to the inverted columns in Michelangelo's Laurentian library.

Terminal B of
Bordeaux Airport

BORDEAUX, 1996

Airports rarely evoke images of serenity and stillness. On the
contrary, they suggest speed and commotion, or perhaps even a
panicky flavor of overly hectic schedules and missed connections.
The unhassled calm inspired by Terminal B at the Bordeaux airport,
therefore, comes as a refreshing surprise.

Paul Andreu, a highly-regarded designer of airports, is an architect
in the richest sense of the classical tradition, a tradition
characterized in part by the search for conceptual clarity and by
the tying of beauty to notions of simplicity and truth. Terminal B of
the Bordeaux airport, which is modest in size and intended
exclusively to handle air traffic between Bordeaux and Paris, is
perhaps the projects where his classical quest is most apparent.

A *significant expansion of Terminal A of the Bordeaux airport was completed in 1987. Despite the competition with air travel posed by the high-speed Paris-Bordeaux TGV (Train à Grande Vitesse) line, the 1987 expansion proved inadequate. Constraints imposed by new safety regulations prevented Terminal A from being further expanded.*

Another terminal, Terminal B, with an initial annual capacity of 1.5 million and readily expandable to 2.5 million, was proposed to handle the traffic with Paris. Terminal B is divided into two levels, with departures above and arrivals below. Passengers have barely 80 meters to walk between the airplane gates and the auto viaduct and taxi stand. The upper floor, the departures lounge, is 80 meters long and 50 meters wide. One end connects to Terminal A, while the other is available for future expansion.

View of the viaduct connecting Terminal B to Terminal A.

Details showing the treatment of the pillars and the roof. The cement pillars are considerably lengthened in cross section, making them more effective in bearing load and at the same time allowing light to pass unobstructed.

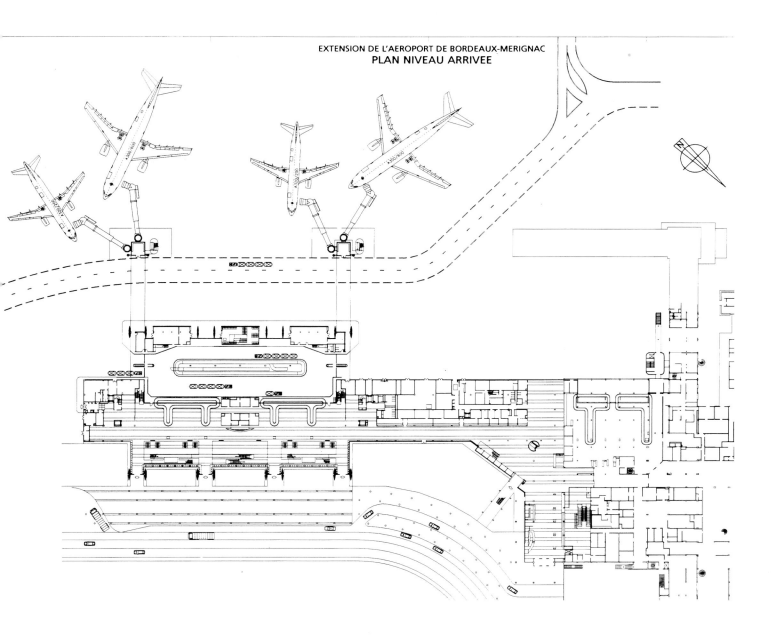

Floor plan of the passenger arrival level.

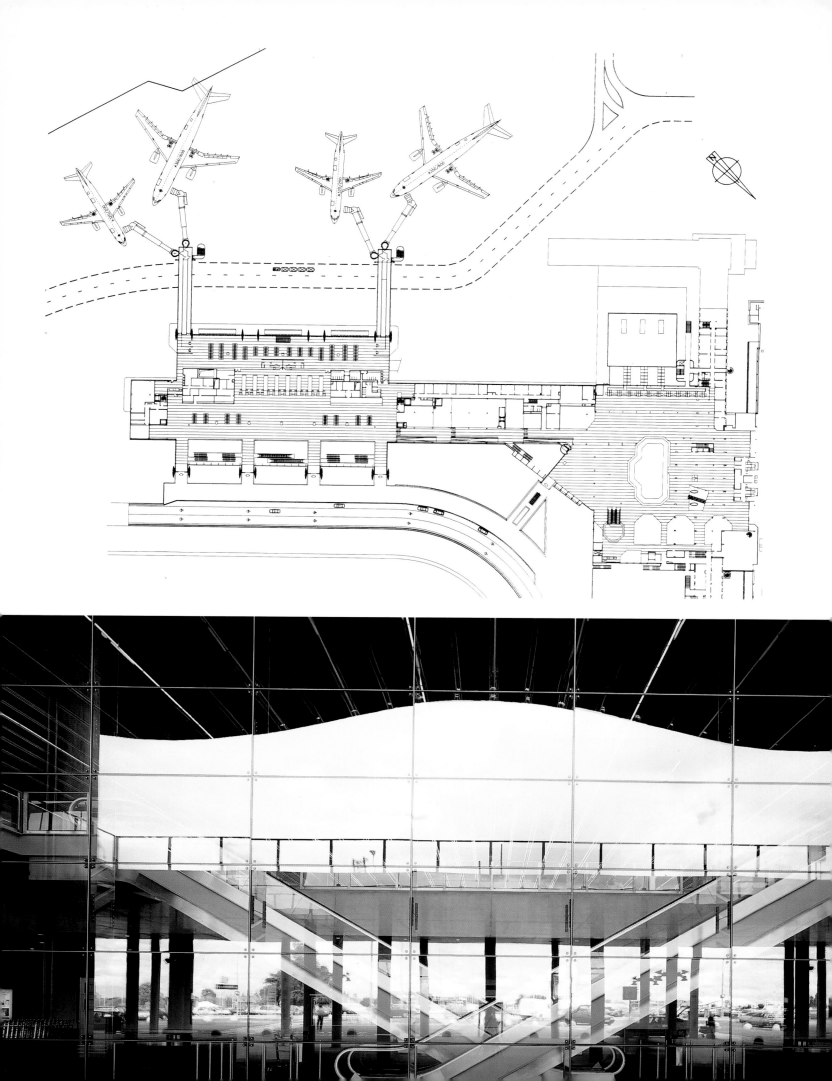

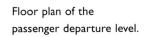

Floor plan of the
passenger departure level.

Views of entry, showing
access to both levels.

The escalators abut with
the façade.

The lower floor receives
ample sunlight through
floor-to-roof glass.

Views of the inside and outside
of the corridor connecting
Terminals A and B.

Baggage retrieval area.

Pointe à Pitre Airport

GUADELOUPE, 1996

Paul Andreu designed the Pointe à Pitre airport only a year after he designed Terminal B at Bordeaux. During that same period, he and his collaborators carried out major projects for airports in Oslo, Manila, Hiroshima, the expansion at Orly, the interchange module at the Charles de Gaulle airport, as well as other commissions not related to transportation.

Such prolific creative output has meant that for Andreu airport design has perhaps become almost a matter of abstraction. His designs for buildings in Paris, Djakarta, Brunei—and at the airport in Guadeloupe—are concrete expressions of an abstraction. For Andreu, in other words, design has become a deductive rather than inductive process as it is for most architects.

Perhaps the driving idea around which Andreu has designed—or deduced—the Pointe à Pitre airport is the notion of light, the most incorporeal element of all. He has adroitly used this idea to unify the entire design. Vertical steel trusses around the perimeter of the building act as a brise-soleil, which creates patterns of light that change throughout the course of the day. The floor itself becomes a screen on which light and shadow play.

The passenger services area runs the length of the building, separating it into two large lounge spaces. This service area acts as a backbone channeling electrical and heating, ventilation, and airconditioning installations, which then branch out at intervals. This scheme allows for shorter conduits and helps reduce energy and installation costs. The double-height space between the three floors provides a series of oblique views linking different parts of the building. Natural light reaches the entire interior.

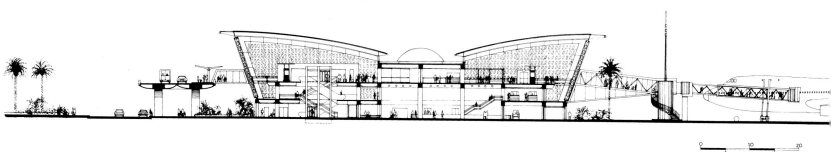

View of the terminal from the runway, showing the striking impression created by the two dramatically curved roofs which open the building up both toward the runways and toward the light.

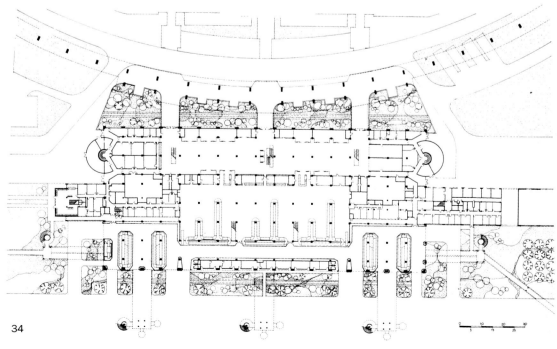

34

View of the front façade of the building as seen from the parking area.

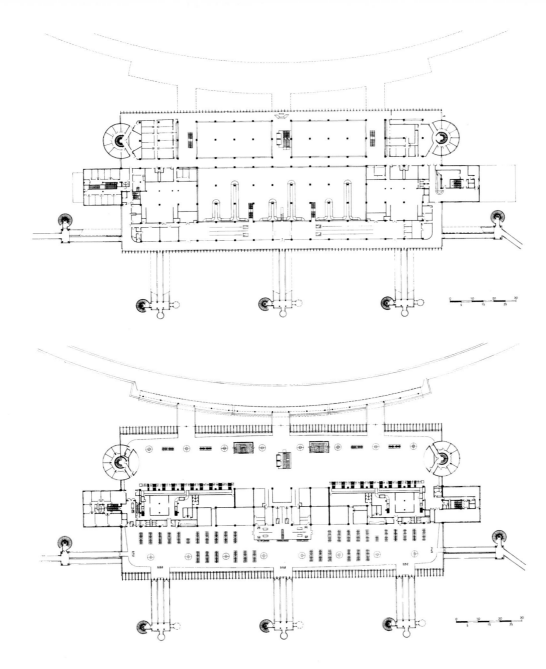

The patterned, metallic exterior facing covering the windows of the large upper-level halls acts to filter and reflect sunlight, creating ever-changing shadows on the floor throughout the day.

The high-ceiling space of the
arrivals lobby is part of
the interplay between
levels that visually unifies
the interior of the building.

Lille Airport

L ILLE, 1996

Denis Sloan, who began flying small aircraft at the age of fifteen in Morocco, has a sincere, undying passion for aviation. Partly because of that passion, perhaps, he detests sterile and impersonal airport terminals. After all, an airport is for many travelers the gateway to exciting destinations and hard-earned adventure. That gateway should itself certainly not be banal or uninspiring.

The fact that an airport must fulfill certain functions should not extinguish the sense of the beauty of airplanes and traveling. As much as possible, airports should reflect the joy and thrill of flying.

Sloan prefers to work with aviation-related architectural themes. His profiles are aerodynamic, and the building materials he chooses are often polished and brilliant. Before an office annex had even been planned, he proposed building one. His idea was to build it along the eastern edge of the terminal in a triangular shape. From a distance, it suggests the tail of an airplane.

The main lounge is six meters above runway level, and the departure gates are at the same height as the planes. Not only does this make boarding planes more convenient, it also gives passengers a more dramatic view over the runway. The main lounge is built around a line of triangular skylights, which illuminates the center of the building. Without these skylights, this portion of the building would be without natural light. The line of light created by the skylight divides the lounge into two functional areas. Airline offices are placed along the line itself, while the departures area is to the west and arrivals to the east. The lower level of the terminal is reserved for passenger services.

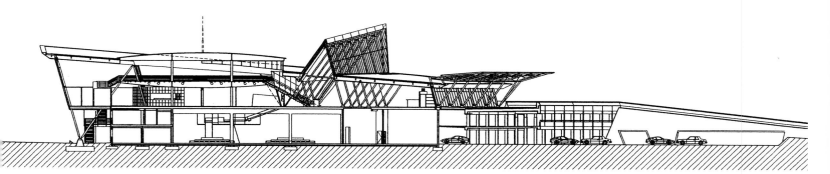

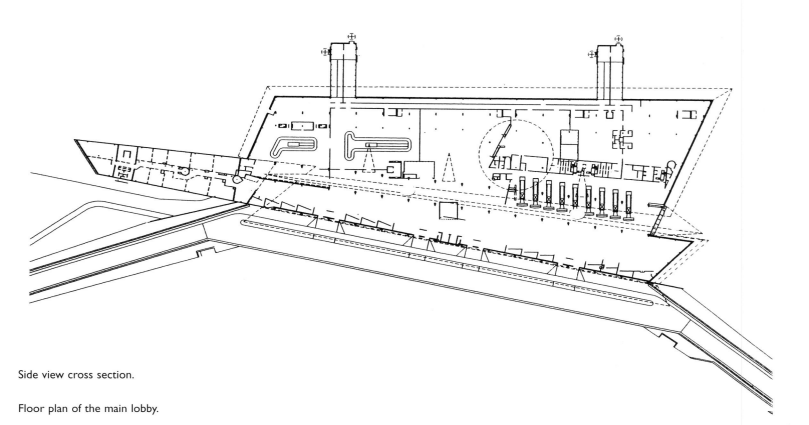

Side view cross section.

Floor plan of the main lobby.

The interior is organized around
a line of large skylights.

West terminal and Plaza at Schiphol

SCHIPHOL, 1993

In his book Los hijos del limo, Mexican author Octavio Paz defines modernity as a process of a continual esthetic revolution that implies a constant negation of the immediate past. Paradoxically, this impulse always to be innovative and different has itself become almost a tradition.

The design of Terminal 3 at Schiphol was inspired by the O'Hare terminal in Chicago. That terminal was innovative in its time because of its generously glassed façades and its departure lounge raised over the runways to allow passengers waiting for flights to watch the planes on the runways. This idea has subsequently become widespread. One of the most poetic seductions of airports is obviously that of watching planes taking off and landing.

The first phase of the new airport dates from 1967. Terminal 3 replaces an older nearby airport, named Schiphol Oost, or East Schiphol. Two years after the completion of Terminal 3, a new twist on the O'Hare theme was added: a shopping plaza in the central triangle between the terminals. Schiphol Plaza serves not only as the principal connector between the two terminals, it also leads to the passenger rail facilities.

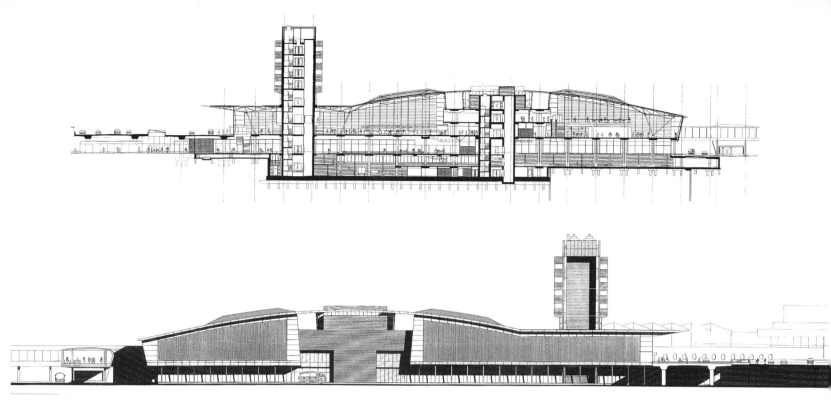

Cross section and elevation of the terminal.

Several images of Schiphol Plaza, a commercial center adjoining the terminal, and open since 1995. The center houses more than forty businesses, including restaurants, bars, stores, bank offices, and car rental companies.

The principal idea is to endow the airport with a business center that has an urban character and appearance, and which can conveniently accommodate the pedestrian traffic generated by airline passengers.

To unify Terminal 3 functionally with the older terminal, and to preserve a sense of a single terminal, an 80-meter-long corridor connects them. The new building is 150 meters long, divided into three sections of 50 meters. By adding more of these 50-meter sections, future expansions could extend the building up to 350 meters further. The lobby has a large curved roof made of steel plate, supported by strutwork that become white-lacquered pillars as they reach the floor. The triangular sections formed by the strutwork housed skylights.

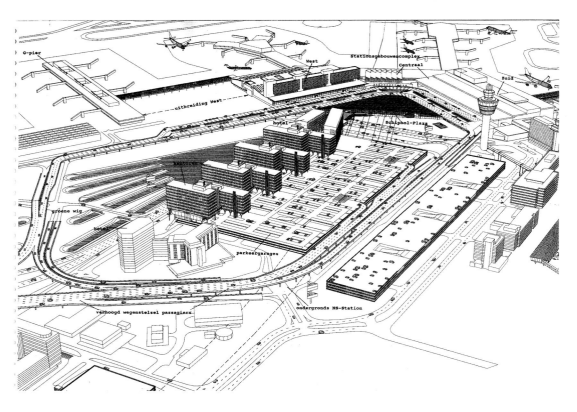

G-pier
West
Stationsgebouwencomplex
Centraal
Zuid
uitbreiding West
hotel
Schiphol-Plaza
kantoren
groene wig
hotel
parkeergarages
verhoogd wegenstelsel passagiers
ondergronds NS-Station

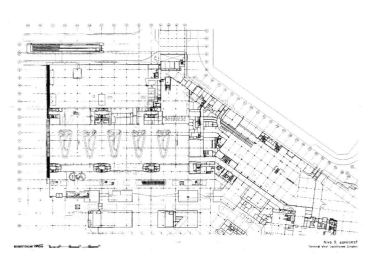

Nivo 0, aankomst
Terminal West Luchthaven Schiphol

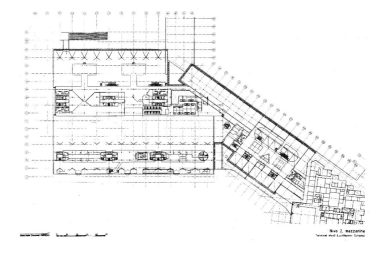

Nivo 2, mezzanine
Terminal West Luchthaven Schiphol

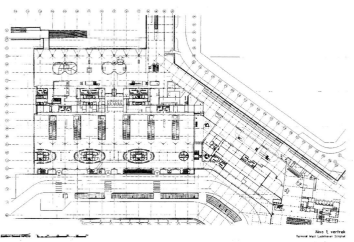

Nivo 1, vertrek
Terminal West Luchthaven Schiphol

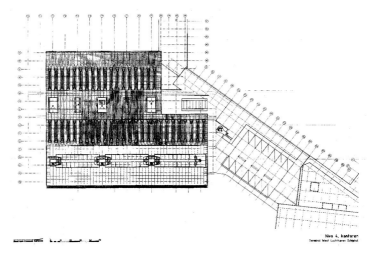

Nivo 4, kantoren
Terminal West Luchthaven Schiphol

Floor plans of Terminal 3.

Views of the interior of the
departures lobby.

Detail of the Nautilus restaurant
designed by Nigel Coates.

Hamburg Airport

HAMBURG, 1993

Perhaps because of their immense cost and scope, airports tend to grow in an organic, disorganized manner through successive additions, in a way resembling the structures of living things. If done successfully, buildings will appear to metamorphose, as new buildings are added without demolishing existing ones. However, this is extraordinarily difficult to accomplish, as in the analogy of building an aircraft while also flying in it.

One of the most complex tasks in architecture is to give new form to what already exists. In the case of airports, that task means not only renovating or expanding existing buildings, but also creating an overall image. After many expansions and modifications, the esthetics of an airport can grow muddled. Sometimes what is needed is to examine and then reform the overall idea, not merely to add another corridor to the labyrinth, but to enforce some kind of order.

The main design principles for the Hamburg airport, which were originally set out in 1986, remain relevant today. The spine, or unifying element, of the complex is the aircraft pier, which swings to the west at its northern end to allow later expansion for three additional buildings and also to bring the end of the long, asymmetrical building to an acceptably harmonious close. This overall design for the airport integrates the old with the new, and ensures ample flexibility for orderly expansion.

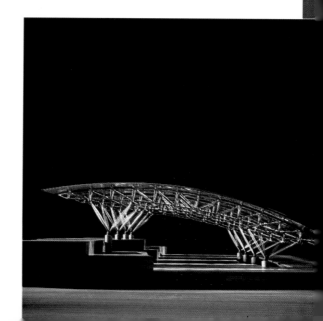

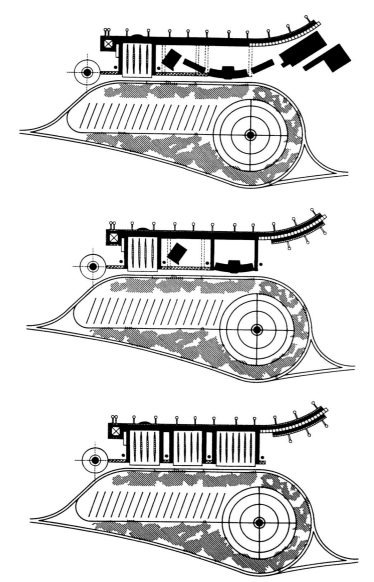

The roof covers an area of 75 by 101 meters with seven triangular roof trusses. The roof loading is spread over diagonal split pairs of columns onto 12 pre-stressed concrete pillars. It is light and relatively inexpensive in spite of its 62-meter span, and is constructed as a single element without expansion joints. The roof counteracts the wind loading of the façade by using split columns and is free standing. The steelwork remains visible, only painted.

The essential architectural problems are the same in the Hamburg terminal as in a Gothic cathedral: achieving an imposing, empty space, harnessing natural lighting, and creating a formal expressiveness for the structure.

One of the fundamental questions in the project concerned integrating the existing long corridor with the boarding areas.

The arrivals lounge is located on the ground floor, and the departures hall on the upper floor.

Shot of the façade of one of the office blocks flanking the lobby, with the ventilation tubes in the foreground.

In the cross-sections and elevations the stepped structure of the building can be appreciated, as well as the importance of the boarding corridor as axis and nexus for the airport's successive expansions.

Perforated sheeting filters light on the stairwell.

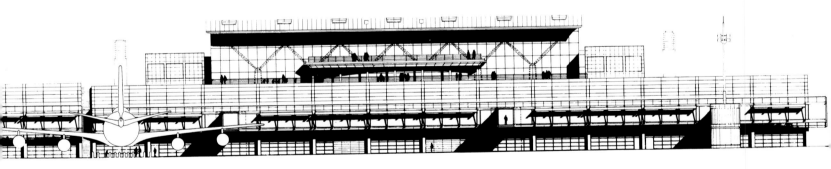

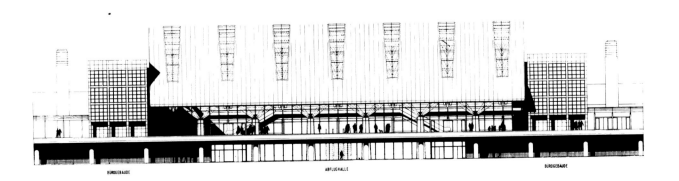

BÜROGEBÄUDE   ABFLUGHALLE   BÜROGEBÄUDE

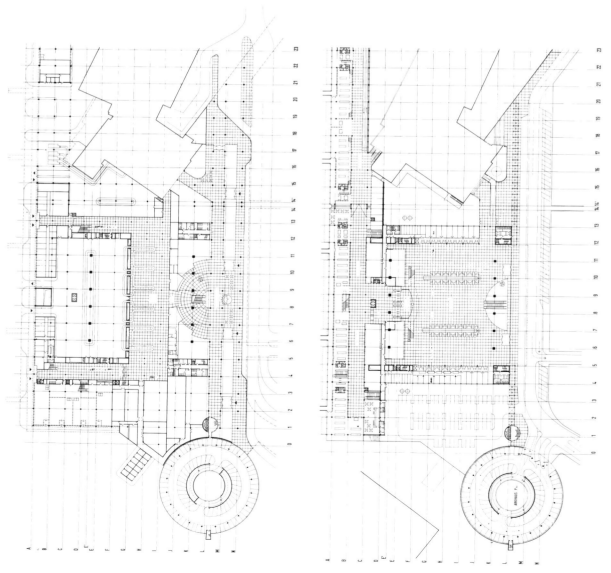

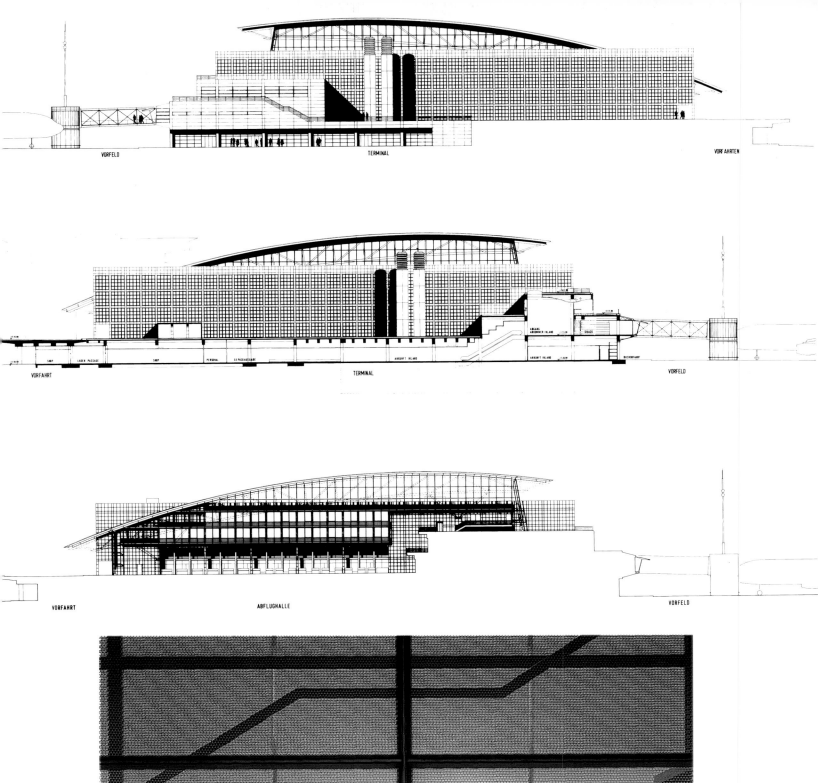

VORFELD   TERMINAL   VORFAHRTEN

VORFAHRT   TERMINAL   VORFELD

VORFAHRT   ABFLUGHALLE   VORFELD

The detailed finish of the supporting structure, the stairs, ventilation tubes, and the luggage conveyor belts, allows a purely functional building with many industrial elements to convey a painstaking, elegant image.

The parking building is the first ever built by von Gerkan for the Hamburg airport. However, the stairways and circular ramps are one of the recurring themes throughout all the works of Meinhard von Gerkan and, perhaps, one of the most suggestive.

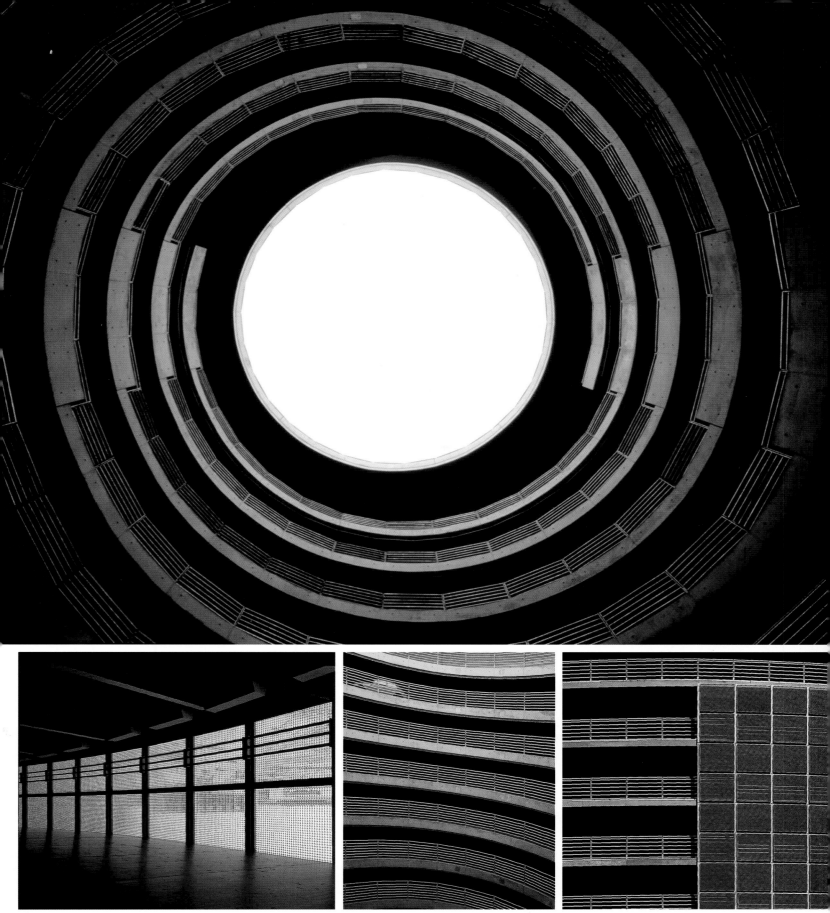

Stansted, Stuttgart, and Köln:
The Airport as Forest

Incorporating figures from nature into buildings, such as mountain ranges at the Denver airport or birds at the Lyon-Satôlas station, is not a new phenomenon in architecture. Rather, it is cyclical. Images of plantlife played a role in classicism, as well as in the art nouveau doors and balustrades of Gaudí and Horta.

The idea of portraying the supporting pillars of a building as trees, or the roof as foliage, is a metaphor so ancient that it may even precede architecture itself.

The metal forests seen in airports at Stansted, Stuttgart, and Cologne not only reply to this image, but also transform buildings associated with the highest of today's technologies into symbols that reflect a yearning for a closer relationship with nature.

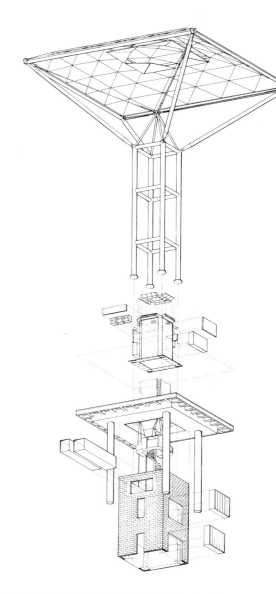

The Stansted airport, near London, was built by Norman Foster in 1990.

The roof is a network of six-by-six-meter steel tubes which inscribe modules having a repeating pattern. At the center of each rectangle of three-by-three modules is a tree of pillars, each bifurcating into four tubes and forming the node of a network.

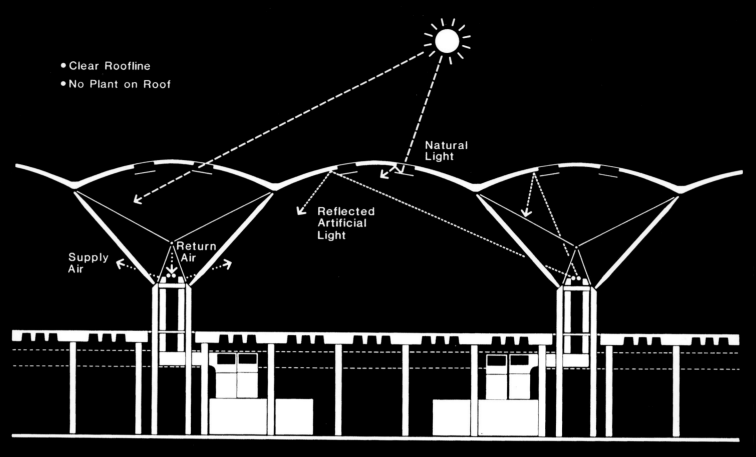

- Clear Roofline
- No Plant on Roof

Natural Light

Reflected Artificial Light

Supply Air

Return Air

- Floor Mounted Plant
- Easy Access

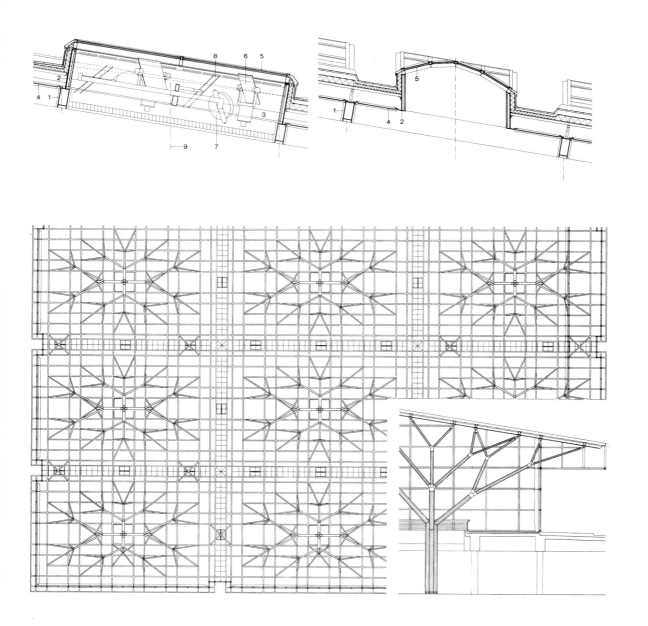

Lobby of the airport terminal at Stuttgart, designed by Meinhard von Gerkan in 1992.

Detail of the roof, which allows as much natural light to enter the building through skylights as is provided by artifical light coming from the housings.

The sloped roof and the stepped platforms at various levels of the lobby introduce an underlying feeling of movement, in an image that has been compared to the mythical forest portrayed in Shakespeare's Macbeth.

So that the roof can better be appreciated, von Gerkan had the ventilation ducts mounted on ticket counters and elevator houses.

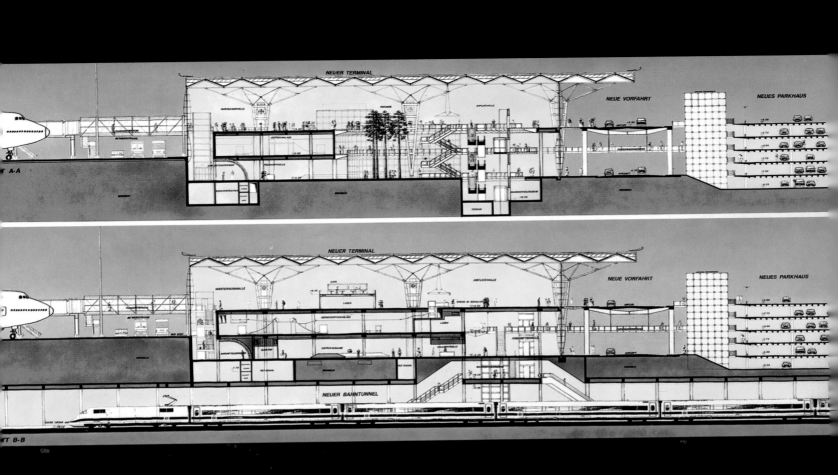

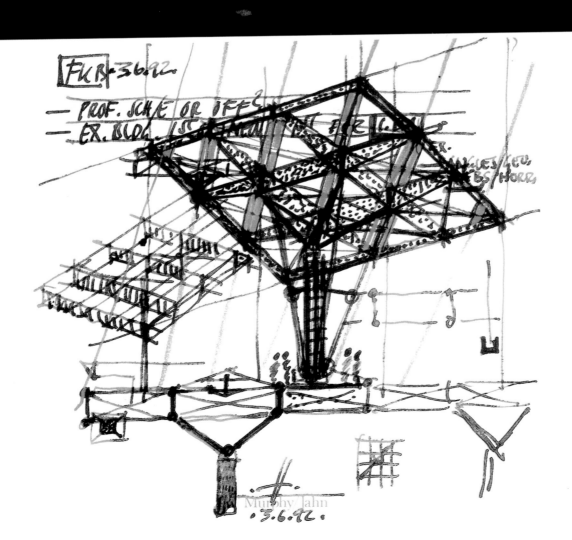

Train Stations

The nineteenth century was the century of the train. In those days, it wasn't just the principal means of long distance transport, but was also one of the main motors for industry and the paradigmatic symbol of technicality.

In this century, trains have been used by an infinitely greater number of passengers. Nevertheless, the appearance of other means of transportation, cars and planes generally, has diluted symbolic character their.

Now, at the gates of the twenty-first century, the railroad is changing its use. On the one hand, in many countries construction has begun on a second network given over to high-speed trains (300 Kmph). These new lines are linked to airports (two cases are presented in this book: the Lyon-Satôlas airport station and those at Paris-Charles de Gaulle), so that the train now becomes an extension of the plane and not an alternative.

On the other, with the movement of population out from the centers of cities and towns towards the suburbs, the train has become the linking component between the residential periphery and the commercial and financial center. In this case, the majority of users of the line make the journey daily, hence the station perhaps becoming the most important focal point of the neighborhood.

However, station designers often limit themselves to projecting the building solely considering the organization of passenger flows, and the immediate functional program - without bearing the urban facet in mind. Nevertheless, in some recently constructed suburbs, identical on the whole, the station could actually become one of its differentiating elements, the building capable of contributing a particular image, unlinked from the homogenous mass of alike buildings surrounding large towns or cities, and, thus, become a sign of the locality's identity. This urbanistic preoccupation is the origin of the projects for the stations at Solan Beach, Sandvika and Sabadell.

The large, vaulted structures of glass and steel, the express wagons stationed at the platforms and the last, urgent kiss of farewell; the small village station sporting a large-lettered sign, a clock and an anonymous building, the station chief and the passenger getting off the train and standing there alone: none of these images correspond to a high-speed network or the concept of station as public space. The image of the new stations is still an open-ended one.

The TGV Station at the Airport of Lyon-Satôlas

Lyon, 1996

"My work is more figurative than organic, in the sense that what interests me are specific sculptural-anatomical associations, based always on static examples that are utterly purist. Working with isostatic structures carries you almost inevitably to schemas found in nature."- *Santiago Calatrava*

Located thirty kilometers north of Lyon, the Lyon-Satôlas station is the first to join an airport to a high-speed railway network in Europe. The authorities in the Rhône-Alps region, including the Chamber of Commerce and Industry for Lyon, and SNCF, the national French railroad company, put out a call for bids in 1990 for what they intended to be a prototypical example of meeting an altogether new architectural need. The competition was won by Santiago Calatrava.

In his design for the station, which looks like a sculpture of a bird of prey about to take flight, Calatrava uses two of his favorite compositional devices: symmetry and duality. He has a unique capacity to transmit through form the forces trapped within the physical elements of a building. He can express in an intuitive way the tensions that come together in the material, and thus unfold the poetry intrinsic within it.

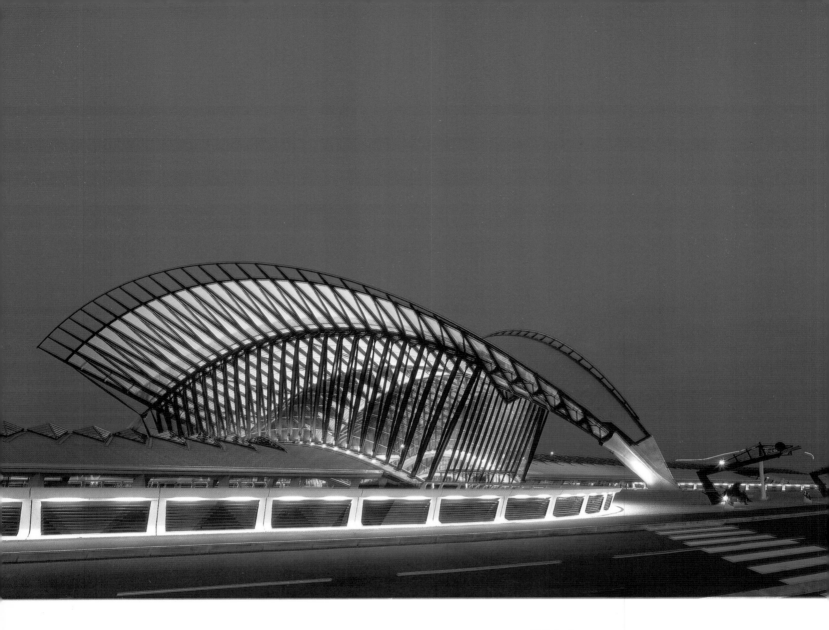

The technical solutions that Calatrava's designs adopt, although extremely sophisticated, seem natural: suggesting animal skeletons, perhaps, or trees. The structures are not designed merely as zoomorphic analogues, however. What is important is that the end result of experiencing them evokes nature.

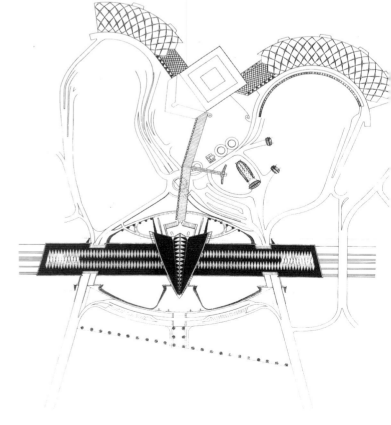

Night and daytime views of the station's main façade. As in so many of his projects, Calatrava employs symmetry as a design element.

Overall floor plan.

The concrete roof over the platform area, almost at ground level. The steel roof traverses almost perpendicularly overhead.

As in the TWA terminal in New York, the building takes on the appearance of a bird, although a bird with a lighter, more ethereal appearance.

Volumetric development of the roof of the lobby area.

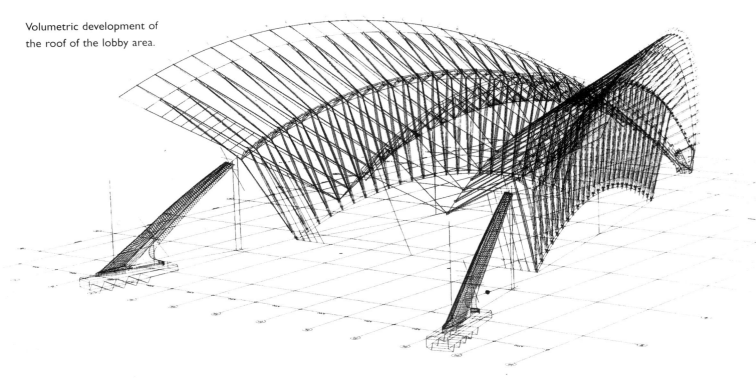

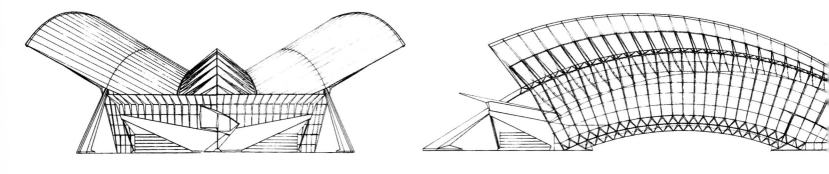

Elevations.

Three means of transport converge on the station: automobiles, airplanes, and trains.

View of the concrete vertex or buttress, facing the entrance.

Cross-section.

Beginning from the concrete
vertex, facing the entrance, two
identical, bifurcating steel arches
define the large triangular space
comprising the main hall.

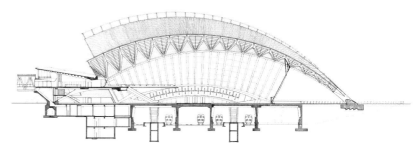

View of the access to the platforms from the lobby. Two roof components intersect over the hall. The lobby's two inside stairways are reminiscent of a bird's foot.

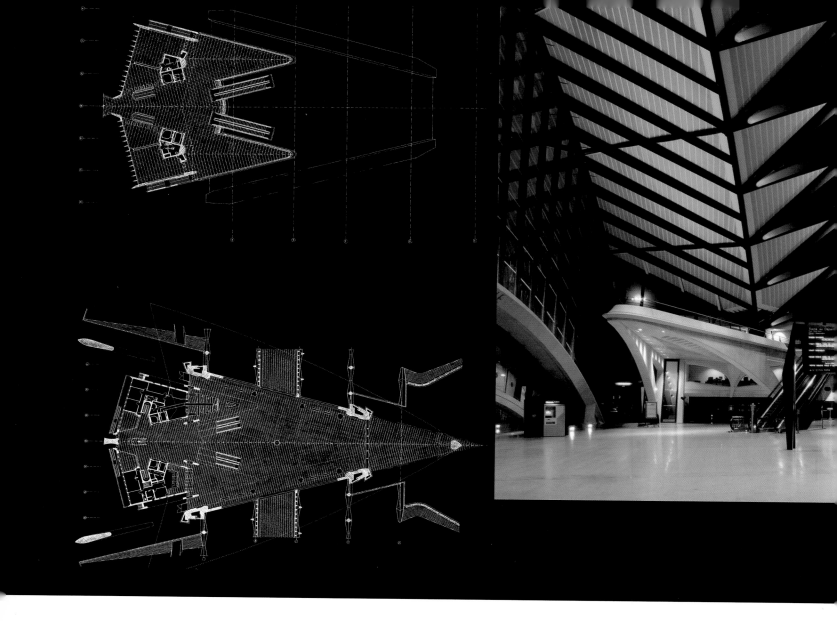

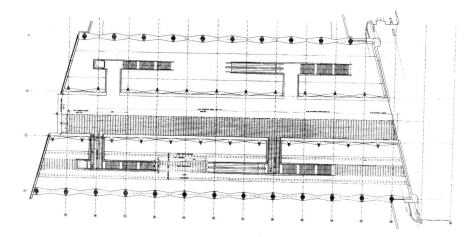

Access floor to the
passenger walkway.

Lobby floor plan.

Platform area floor plan.

The lobby allows passage
over the tracks to the
passenger walkway leading
to the airport's terminal.

The roof over the platforms is built using a network of oblique beams of white concrete.

As in all Calatrava's works, materials are reduced more or less to three: concrete, steel, and glass.

The roof over the
six tracks runs for
half a kilometer.

PAUL ANDREU, J.-M. DUTHILLEUL

Charles de Gaulle Airport Interchange Module

PARIS, 1994

Blaise Pascal explains in one of his writings that the infinite and the infinitesimal are reflections of each other, that the macrocosm and microcosm are alike and possibly even interchangeable. More than an image, this metaphor captures an important aspect of the feeling of that century, the epoch of the invention of the calculus, the variations of Bach, and the architecture of Borromini, with its innumerable folds and paradoxes.

From the air, the Roissy-Charles de Gaulle airport looks remarkably like a living organism, as if it were a protozoan being examined under a microscope. Perhaps this immense transportation center truly is alive; since its beginning it has undergone continuous growth and transformation. Roissy inspires this type of emotion. Some of its occupants weigh hundreds of tons and measure tens of meters—airplanes. Trains, airplanes, automobiles, and people move in parallel, sometimes barely crossing paths and fusing completely.

In Roissy, architecture finds itself at a threshold, on the point either of falling or of becoming transfigured. This is a place both complex and suggestive at the same time, perhaps explaining the feeling of a certain century, as well.

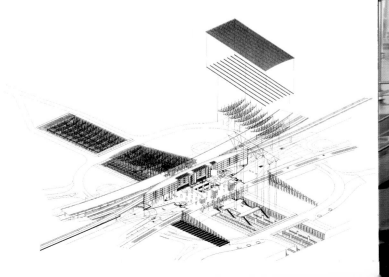

Plan showing growth of the Charles de Gaulle airport.

Several images of Terminal 2.

Cross sections and an axonometric drawing of the interchange module and of the hotel.

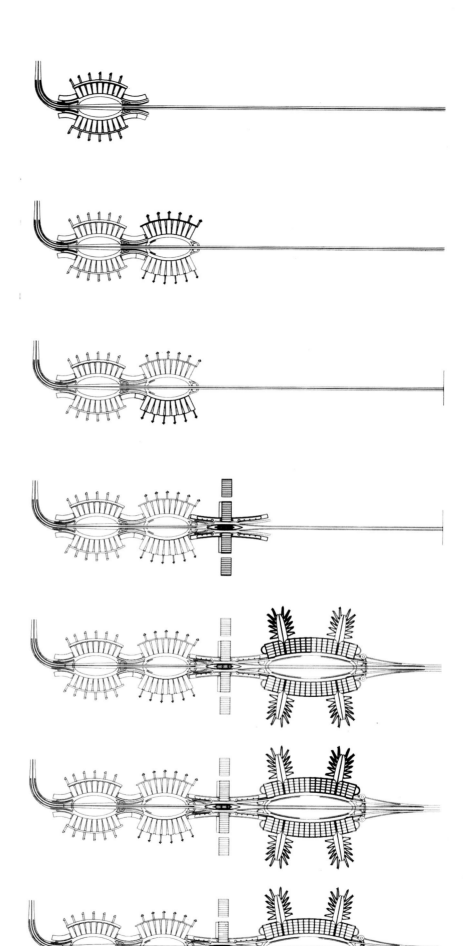

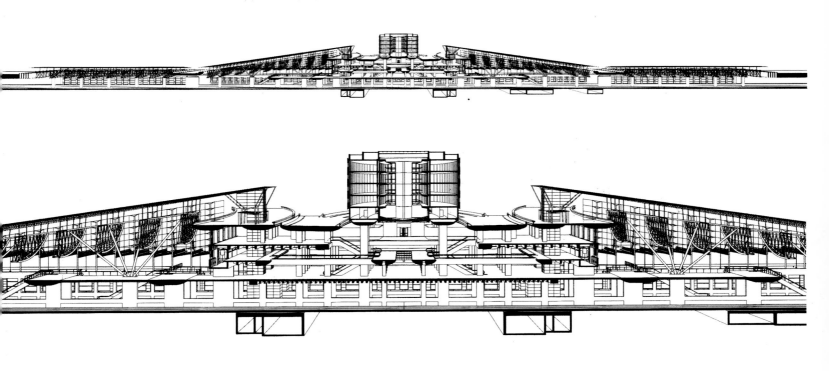

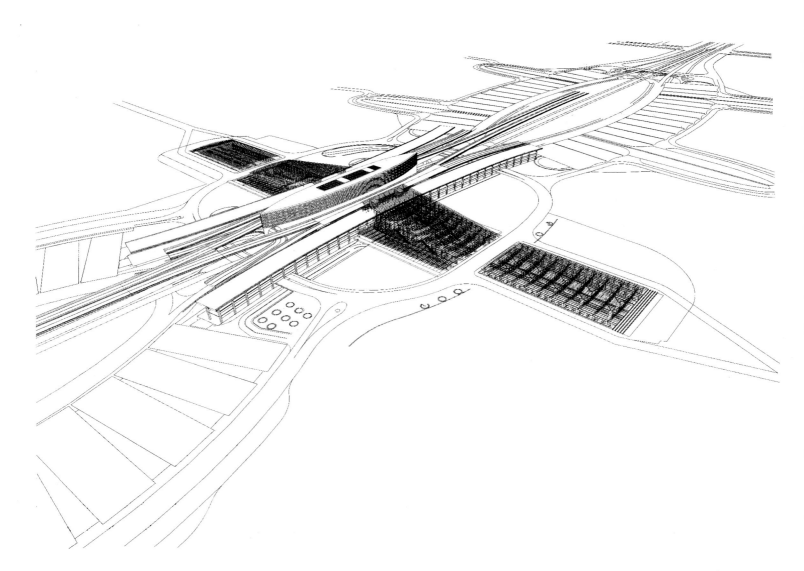

The hotel has been built along the axis of growth of the airport.

The TGV, or high-speed rail, station in the Roissy-Charles de Gaulle airport is integrated into Terminal 2 as an interchange module. The module will become the center of the airport as it is completed. Apart from the advantages accrued by maintaining certain installations in common, this connection between rail and air networks makes connections impressively convenient. Because Roissy connects with other major French and European cities through the rail system, the airport serves a much larger population.

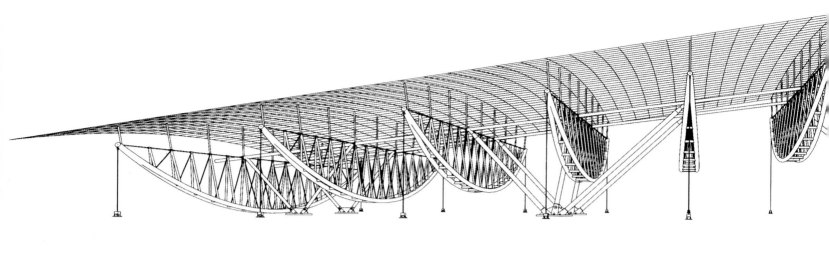

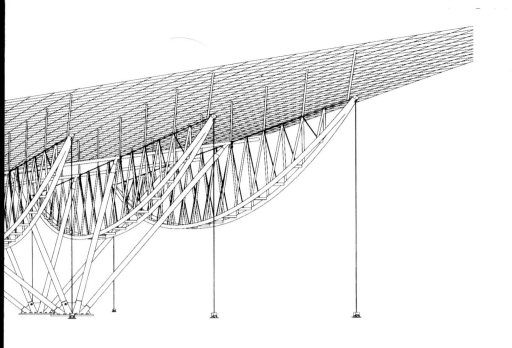

Paul Andreu had the conviction that the richness and complexity of the place should derive not only from its functionality, but also from its poetry.

"We think that it would be a good idea to locate the thickest part of the structure as low as possible with respect to the level of the windows, and that the structure become thinner as it goes higher. In this way, when the eye reaches the roof, the structure hardly exists at all, having become seemingly transparent. That's the idea behind the inverted lattices." Paul Andreu (in an interview with Serge Salat and Françoise Labbé)

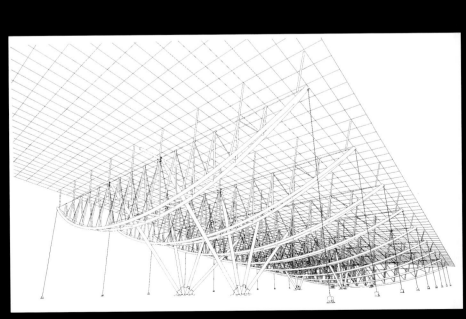

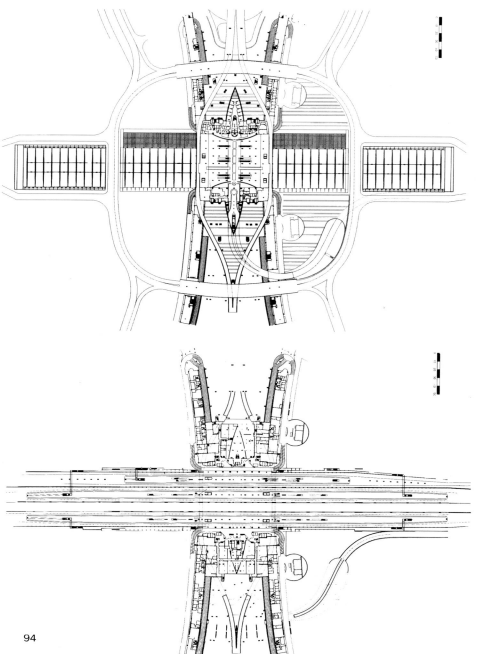

"My intent was to impart to travelers the sensation of passing through a vast structure, a composition that unfolds like music, with forms and emotions opening up one after another without repeating and yet without becoming too familiar. The mental image ought to be global, while the pleasure the image gives should be immediate and changing."

View of the lobby level and of the platform level.

Slependen Station

BAERUM, 1993

Certain traditional Japanese gardens offer a unique experience to each visitor. The visitor is guided through the paths in a particular way. The landscaper of the garden has planned each moment of the visitor's experience carefully, so that the view that the visitor has of the garden and of its buildings changes continually according to position and angle. In this way, the very footsteps of the visitor are what drives the unfolding of the experience.

Le Corbusier had a similar vision when he designed the famous Ville Savoye. He defined the house as *une promenade architecturale* (an architectural walkway). Le Corbusier wanted to create a flow of architectural experiences starting from a walkway and moving across a circuit of ramps and stairways where the simple sculptural forms of its architecture were continuously revealed in various ways.

In the Slependen Station in Baerum, a town on the outskirts of Oslo, an opportunity arose for creating one of these architectural walkways. The terrain was highly dramatic, thanks to the steep slopes and the variety of levels surrounding the site. In order to connect all the existing entries with the platforms, ramps and stairways had to be built. With this as a point of departure, Hendriksen had the chance to create a variety of architectural rhythms and movements.

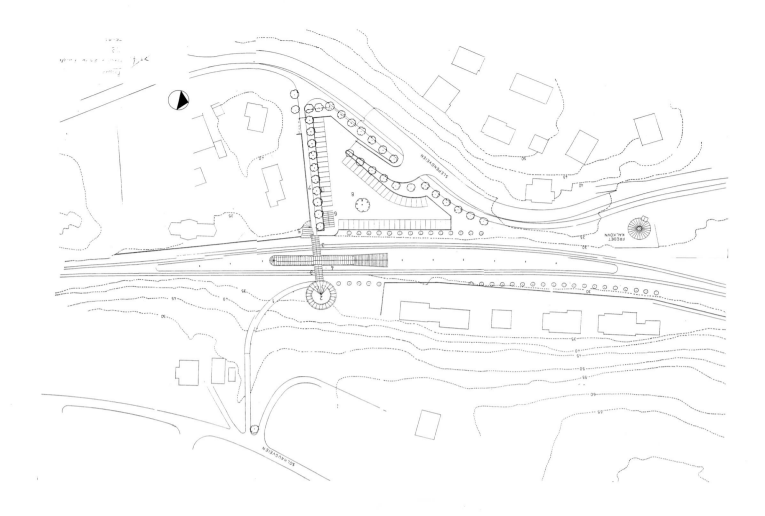

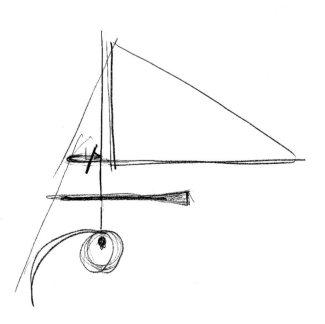

The difference in height between each
side of the track makes bridges, ramps,
and stairways unavoidable.

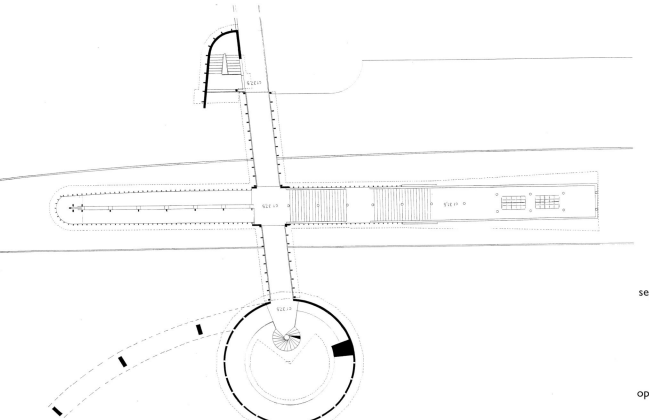

The bridges unite the buildings, which are separate structures built in distinct shapes out of different materials. Inside views of the rotunda. Light enters through the narrow openings between the slabs of prefabricated cement.

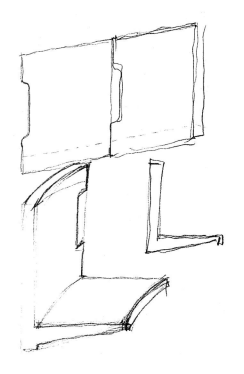

The station has several elements: two ramps, one straight and the other curved, a rotunda, a staircase, a ramp-stairway, and two bridges. Each of these elements has its own individual architecture, with its own materials and appearance. The overall impression given by the buildings seems inherited from the native architecture of Norway, with its heavy wooden posts and beams. In the design of Slependen, cement represents heaviness, while the wooden structures constitute the lighter and more active parts. In this landscape, the building presents a stern, austere, but serene face.

Not exceptionally intricate or technological, the structures are engineered out of wood and roughly-surfaced cement.

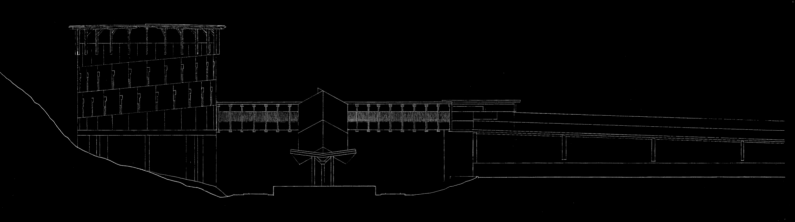

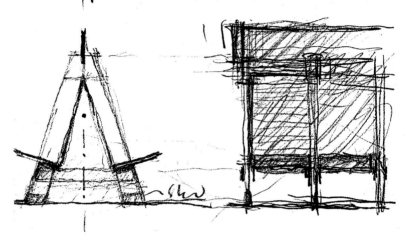

*egment, byggindustidesign.
Definigon av AHO. - Tydligere!
Mangel på refleksjon i diplomen.?*

Image of the platforms. The benches have unusually high backs.

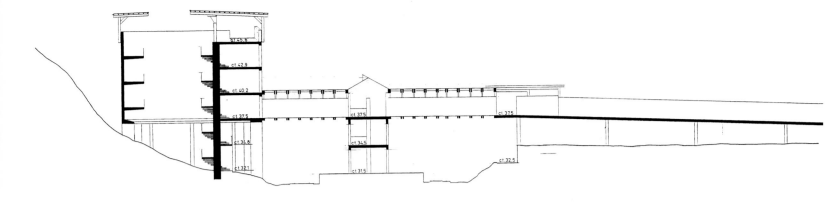

The wooden structure
acts as a sort of Venetian
blind.

Sandvika Station

SANDVIKA, 1994

Sandvika, located about 15 kilometers south of Oslo, is at the center of a community of about 70,000. Connections to Oslo play an immensely vital role in the life of this community. The new train station is part of a larger project intended to improve transportation between Sandvika and Oslo, and also to revitalize the business section of Sandvika.

The tracks cross Sandvika at an elevation, and basically divide the city in half. The idea suggested by this project was to build the station beneath the rails. In this way, two parts of the town that had formerly been separated are now reunited. The fact that the station is beneath the tracks presents an opportunity for interesting architecture.

City squares serve to integrate the existing parts of the town with the station. The Jernbaneplass, or Station Park, along the eastern side of the station, was conceived as a focal point for the town's pedestrian district. Here is also where the bus lines make connections with the train station.

In the design of Slependen Station, Arne Henriksen develops an architecture based on rotundas, gangways, ramps, and stairways. In Sandvika station, the underlying concept is the same, although its outworking is different.

The tunnel of the station running beneath the tracks serves to unite two sectors of the town that had formerly been separate.

The ceiling of the concrete arch was painted the same white as the city hall. Contrasting with the concrete arch, the wooden ceiling structures are much lighter and friendlier. These wooden structures guide the passenger through the station, from the entrance to the tracks. The floor and walls of the station are dressed with black slate.

The wooden structure serves
not only to protect
passengers from foul weather
as they wait on the platform;
it also formally integrates the
two levels of the station.

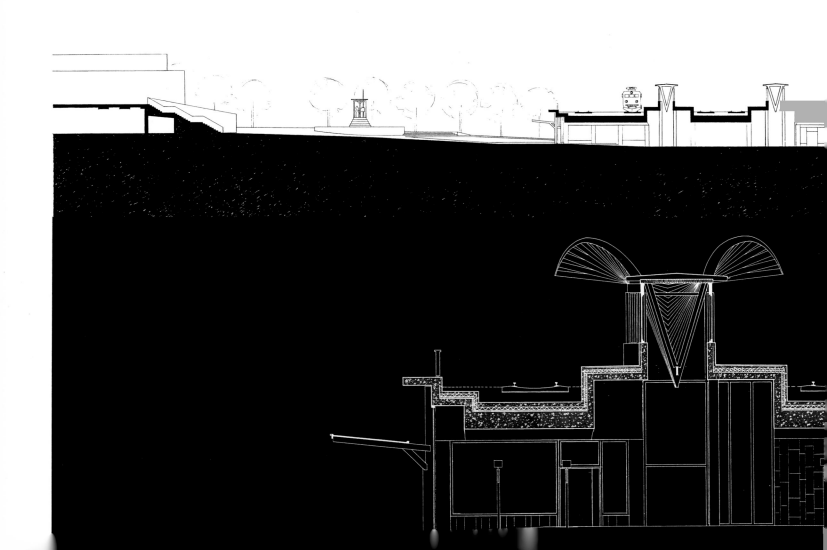

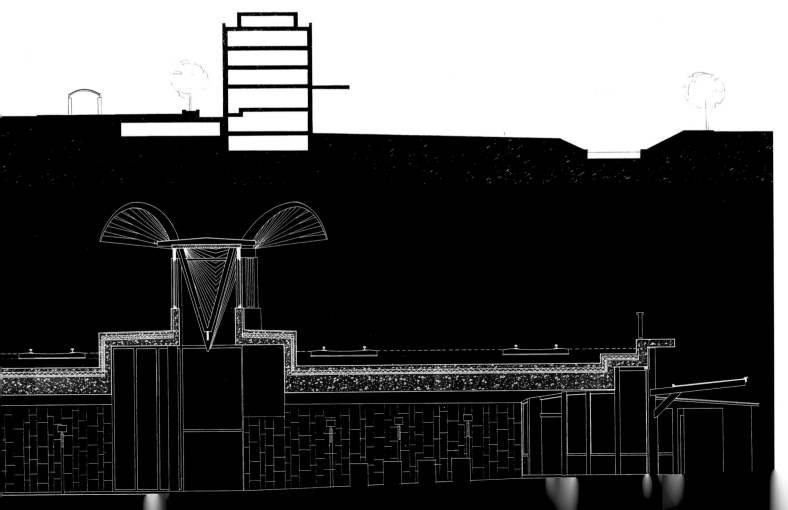

The wooden roof is the
basic element in the design.

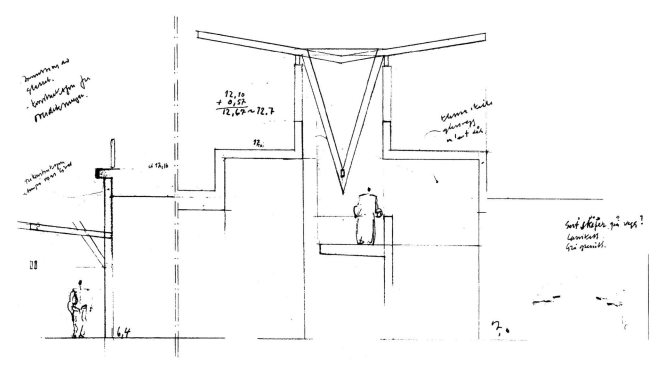

Solana Beach Transit Station

SOLANA BEACH, CALIFORNIA, 1995

Train travel inspires a different relationship with the landscape than does travel by air or in a car. The landscape moves past like a colorful ribbon, winding itself out with a relentless rhythm. The towns with stops along the rail line are relatively unremarkable, especially in Southern California, the very heartland of the automobile. Only the larger cities make a lasting impression. The small towns are just moments of uncomfortable silence as the train stops periodically along its journey—they are distinguishable only by their names. Solana Beach is an exception, however.

According to Rob Wellington Quigley, the unusual design of the station was inspired by two items commonly seen in the area surrounding Solana Beach. One is the World War II–style Quonset huts, a few of which remain because of neighboring San Diego's importance as a naval center. The other inspiration comes from greenhouses. Many of the station's details recall typical European train stations, as well, such as the looming presence of the circular clock. Other elements, however, such as the palm tree grove, have a distinctly Californian flavor.

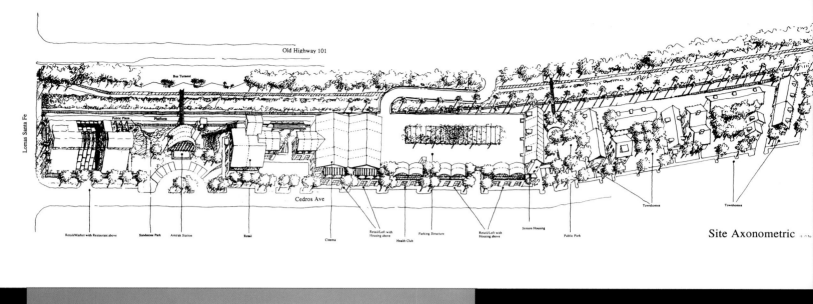

Old Highway 101

Bus Turnout

Public Plaza   Platform

Lomas Santa Fe

Cedros Ave

Townhomes   Townhomes

Site Axonometric

Retail/Market with Restaurant above   Sandstone Park   Amtrak Station   Retail   Cinema   Retail/Loft with Housing above   Health Club   Parking Structure   Retail/Loft with Housing above   Seniors Housing   Public Park

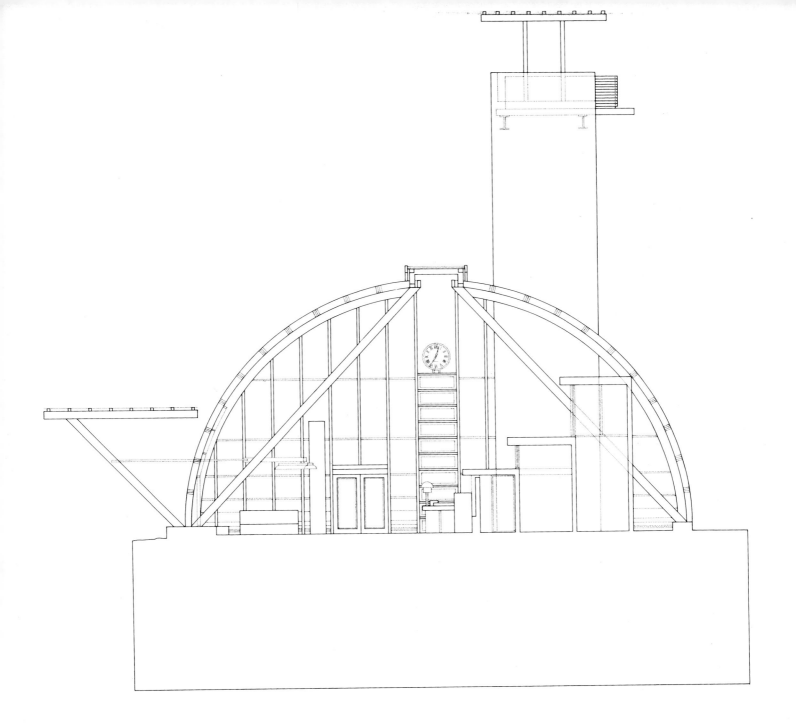

The train station project was the first phase of a larger urban construction project totaling 35,000 square meters, intended to become the new downtown area of Solana Beach during coming years. The entire project was conceived in an unusual way, more open and democratic than usual, because the citizens participated with the architects in designing it. From the very beginning, the city organized workshops in which consensus was sought over the major decisions in the project: traffic flow, parking, acoustic isolation, scale of the construction, and zoning relationships between commercial and residencial buildings.

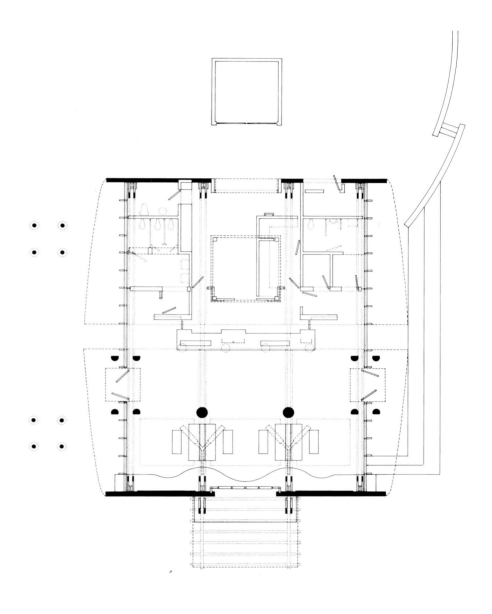

View of the south façade
as seen from the palm
grove, exposing the
structure's rustic
vocabulary.

General plan.

One of the features that emerged from the workshops was that the station should have a tower that made it prominent. In order to do that, a city ordinance had to be changed to allow for a higher maximum height.

Overall veiw of the interior. Interestingly, the entrance is off-center, rather than being positioned beneath the clock.

Detail of the ticket counter. The mountings for the lamps connote an esthetic of spontaneity.

Appearance of the waiting area. The benches are solid concrete.

Sabadell Station

SABADELL, CATALONIA, 1993

Architecturally simple, the Sabadell station was designed with practical considerations in mind. The present station has been built on the same site as a previous, less accommodating station. Before the new station was built, the area in the surrounding neighborhood was unused. In fact, much of the land was taken up by the tracks themselves. The former station divided the city, and Bach and Mora decided that, above all, the new station had to tie the two sectors together again.

Their first decision was to relocate the station slightly and orient it to the surrounding streets. The entrance was aligned with two streets that approached it from the side. Part of the trench for the tracks was covered, and the station was built atop it. In front of the station a tree-lined parking area was built.

Although Sabadell's train station is relatively modest in size, it is intended to have a monumental presence in the city. The architectural elements that make it up, such as the suspended awning, the branched pillars, or the clean lines somewhat reminiscent of Piet Mondrian's paintings, are meant to establish the station as a reference point in a district of the city that is generally incoherent and unappealing.

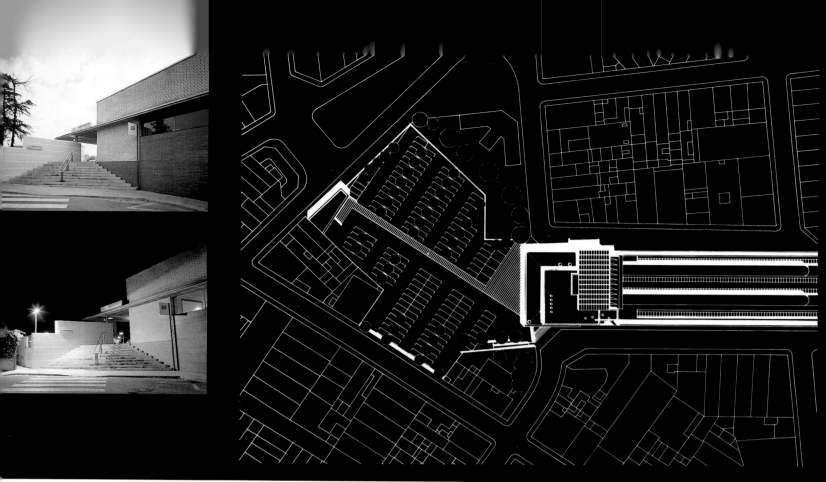

Layout of the site.

At night, the awning is illuminated from beneath, making it prominently visible in the surrounding district.

Detail of entrance with ramp suitable for access by the physically disabled.

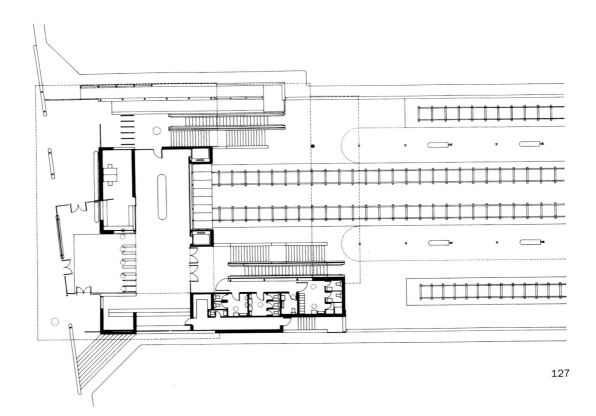

View of the lobby.

Floor plan of the station.

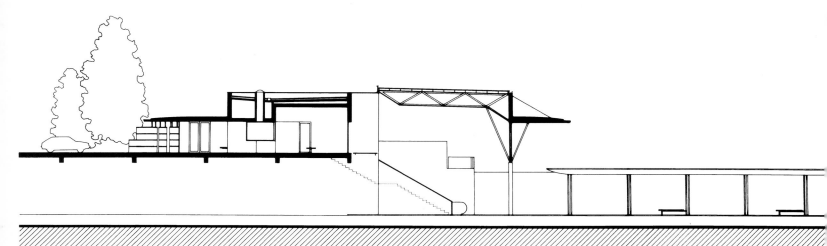

While the Sabadell station is the final stop on the commuter line to Barcelona, the station was designed not only to accommodate passengers arriving from the larger city, but also for those passengers starting from Sabadell. The stairs leading to the track toward Barcelona are directly in front of the lobby entrance, while the stairs from the arrival platform are tangential to the lobby. In this way, arriving passengers need not cross the lobby, and the paths of passengers do not become entangled.

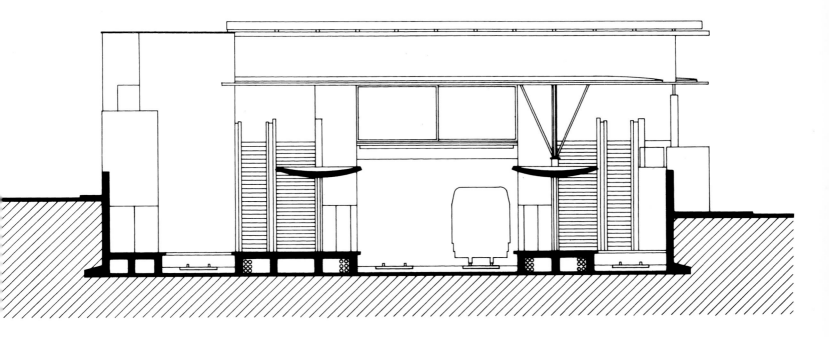

Detail of the awning and the pillars.

Section of the complex.

The entrance to the train station.

View showing escalators with the ubiquitous European train-station clock, and the effective protection from the elements offered by the overhead awnings.

Night view of the concrete overhead shelter covering the platform.

Subway, Streetcar
and Bus:

Urban Transportation

BECAUSE OF THE SUBWAY, CITY DWELLERS ARE ACCUSTOMED TO TRAVELING FROM NEIGHBORHOOD TO NEIGHBORHOOD WITHOUT BECOMING FAMILIAR WITH OR EVEN SEEING THE STREETS IN THOSE NEIGHBORHOODS. THE SUBWAY PASSENGER HAS DIFFERENT A PERCEPTION OF THE CITY. NEIGHBORHOODS ARE NOT CONTIGUOUS, BUT INSTEAD HAVE A TREELIKE STRUCTURE THAT EMERGES FROM A ROOT OR CENTER. THAT CENTER IS THE SUBWAY STATION.

THE SUBWAY STATION IS AN URBAN SPACE JUST AS ARE STREETS, SQUARES, AVENUES, OR PARKS. HOWEVER, A SUBWAY STATION, AS OPPOSED TO OTHER URBAN PLACES, IS STILL NOT SEEN AS A WORTHY HISTORICAL SPACE. THAT VERY LACK OF TRADITION IS WHAT MAKES IT ALL THE MORE ATTRACTIVE TO ARCHITECTS—HERE IS AN EVERYDAY PLACE WAITING TO BE FULLY INVENTED. THE PROJECTS PRESENTED HERE—PLACE DE LA GARE, ALAMEDA, PARILLY, AND BILBAO—EXPERIMENT WITH THESE POSSIBILITIES. FEW URBAN PLACES ARE AS CAPABLE OF UNITING STREETS AND UNDERGROUND GALLERIES, NEOCLASSICAL FAÇADES AND TUNNELS, INTO A SINGLE GLOBAL IMAGE, AS THESE PLACES DO.

BUS AND STREETCAR STOPS ARE TOO OFTEN DESIGNED AS IF THEY WERE MERELY COMMODITIES. THOSE APPEARING ON THE FOLLOWING PAGES, HOWEVER, HAVE BEEN DESIGNED IN TERMS OF THEIR RELATIONSHIP TO THEIR URBAN CONTEXTS. EACH ONE IS INTIMATELY LINKED TO A SPECIFIC SITE—MORE LIKE SCULPTURES THAN JUST A PART OF THE URBAN INFRASTRUCTURE.

Tram station in Strasbourg

STRASBOURG, 1994

Buried in front of the old train station at Place de la Gare lies
Strasbourg's new station, the nexus of the new streetcar system
with which the city government hopes to replace buses and cars.
The new station has connections with principal bus and train lines,
taxis, and also has a parking facility for those passengers who wish
to leave their cars and proceed using public transportation.
The station lies beneath a barren city square. The only portion of
the station visible from the street level is a sunken atrium. Two
simple rows of trees adorn the inside of the atrium, which is
covered by a steel and glass structure. The perimeter of this space
has sites for retail businesses.

Above the escalators and train platforms, the American
artist Barbara Kruger has installed signs on concrete
beams, on which are written in bold letters enigmatic or
confrontational phrases such as, Where are you going?
Who do you think you are? Where is your head? Who has
the last laugh? These messages intermingle with
advertisments and directional signs. At least to the
question of where they are going, most passengers
should have a ready answer.

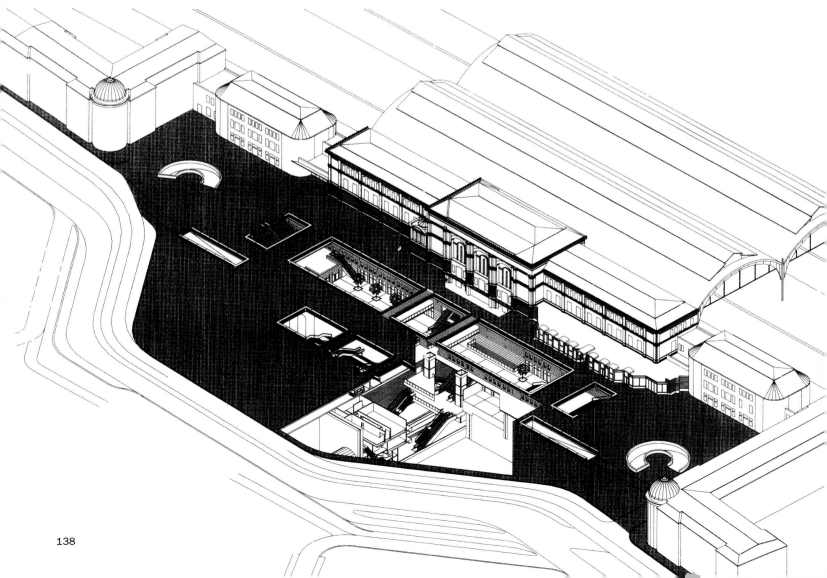

Aerial view of the Place de la Gare, in which can be seen several access points to the station.

Overall view of the atrium with retail shops. This has been conceived as though it were an exterior space. Trees have been planted, and benches and streetlamps installed.

Two images of the impact on the city square had by the immense glass-covered opening to the atrium.

Valente has divided the station into four levels. The two upper levels surround the sunken atrium, which also has pedestrian access to the parking facility on the first underground floor. The platforms for the new subway station are located on the two lower levels. The streetcar enters a 17-meter-deep tunnel beneath the square.

Detail of one of the
access points.

The roof is supported
by load-bearing,
tensioned metal arches
fitted with lighting of the
same length as the width
of the underground
square.

Detail of the stairways.
The walls and pavement
of the square are
covered with grayish-
turquoise Hainaut stone
from Belgium.

The architectural
language used by Gaston
Valente is concise. For
this reason, the steel
structure of the roof
acquires a special
relevance.

Transverse cross-section.

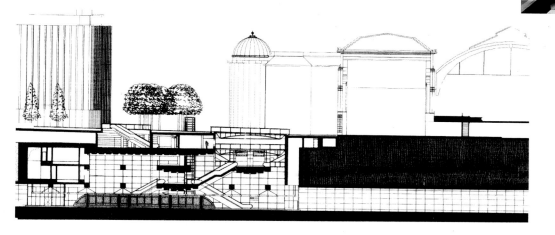

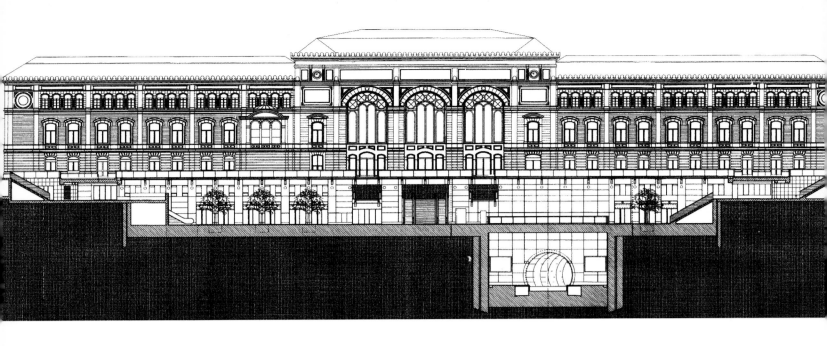

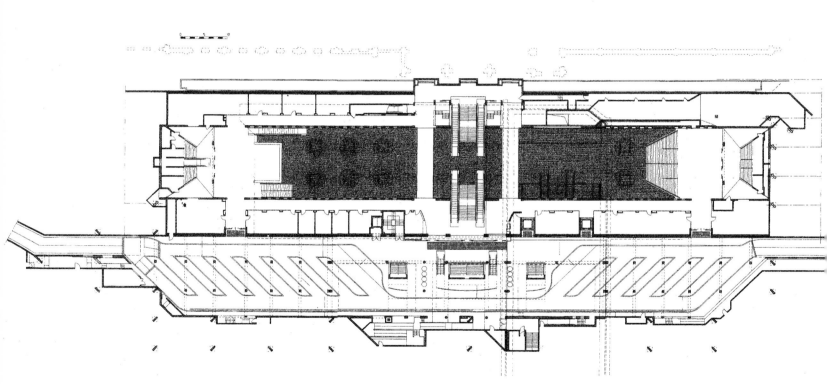

Longitudinal cross-section.

Detail of access area, showing one
of the scripts created by the
American artist Barbara Kruger.

Overall view of the train platform. The materials used are mainly concrete and metal sheeting.

Two views of the underground parking facility showing the use of color as a primary compositional element of this space.

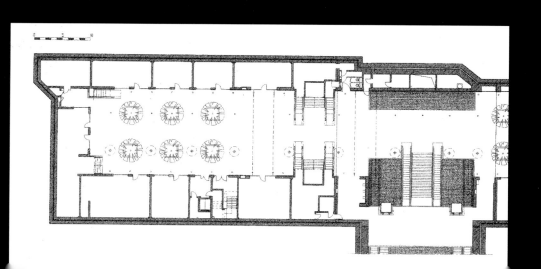

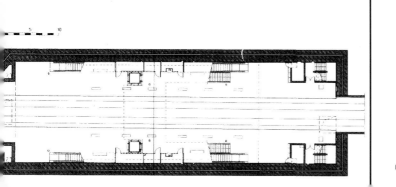

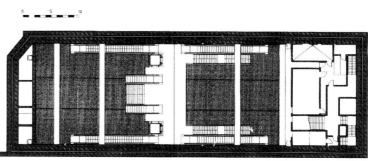

Bilbao Subway

BILBAO, 1996

Norman Foster once remarked that Bilbao struck him as a city with a certain "pleasing harshness." He wanted the new subway to reflect the city's identity as one of Spain's leading industrial centers. He sought to capture Bilbao's industrial feel in his architectural design, which builds upon this image and brings it into harmony with the city's natural surroundings.

The tunnels themselves are a central theme of the design. Foster's stations are cavernous galleries. In his mind, "The tunnel's shape is very powerful-it's such an organic response to natural forces and is so beautifully shaped that it would be a shame to hide it."

Foster strives for a humane, friendly architectural style. His first priority is the public's quality of life. As a result, his designs are noted for their clean appearance, meticulous attention to detail, and generous lighting. A striking example of Foster's approach is his design of the glass and stainless steel shelters covering the subway entrances. At night, they are so well illuminated that they light up the street and serve as clear reference points for pedestrians.

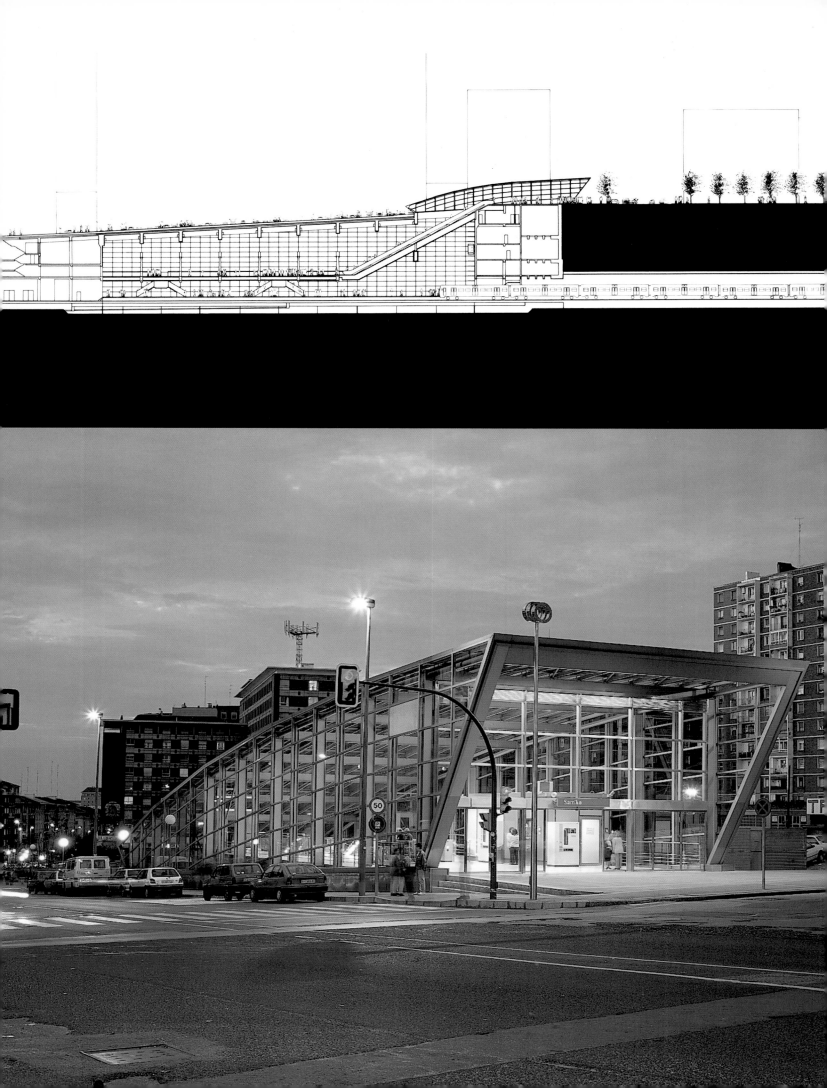

Cross-sections and access
views of the Sarriko station,
one of the most important
stops on the line.

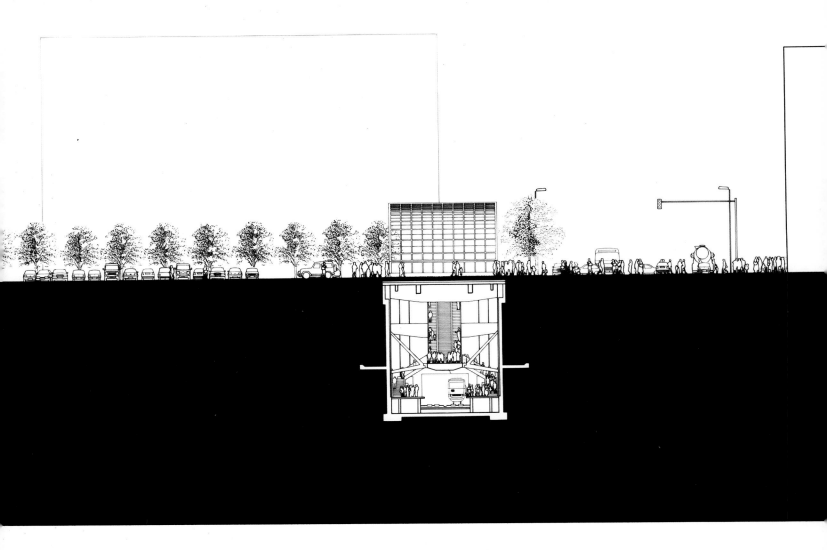

The tunnels are 16 meters wide by 8 meters high, and were built using the New Austrian Tunnel method. Their walls have pre-fabricated, stressed concrete panels measuring 1.2 meters by 2.4 meters. They have been treated with graffiti-resistant material. The project is extensive, and is being completed in stages. Line I has twenty-six stations, with most of the eleven underground sta-tions built out of tunnels. Many of the surface stations are renovations of existing stations. The planned Line II, which will include nine underground stations, will add 20 kilometers (12 miles) to the system.

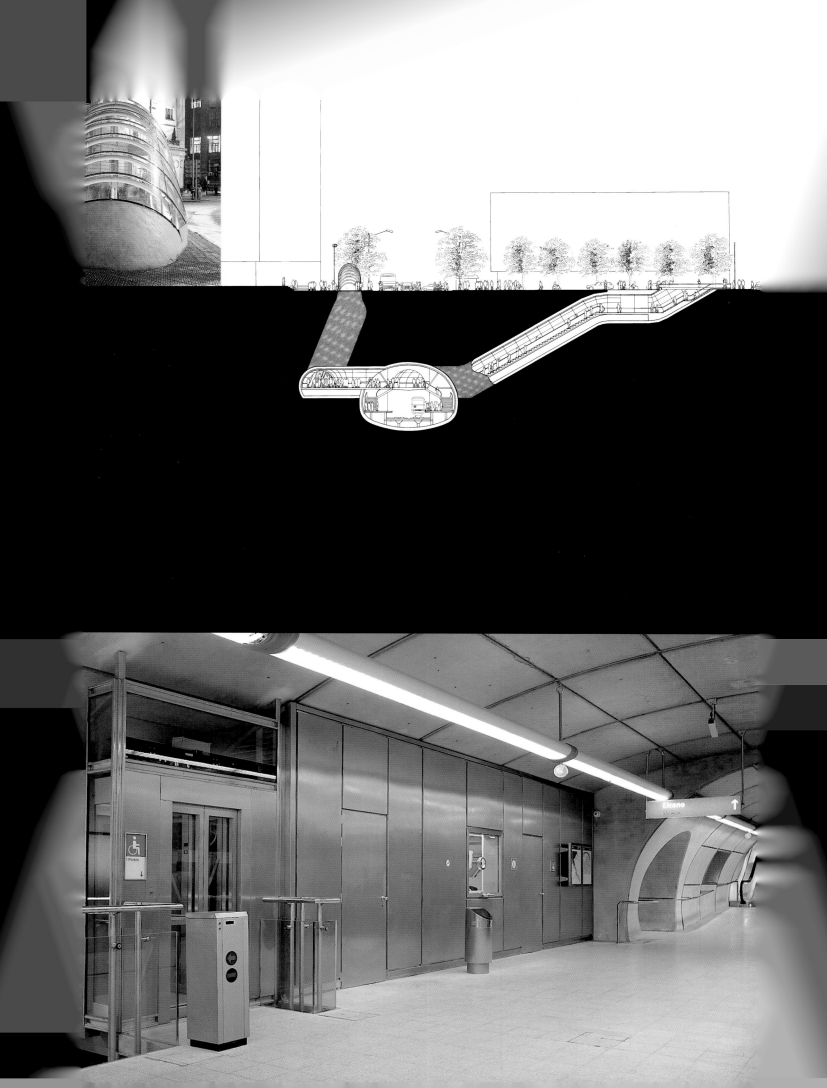

One of Norman Foster's greatest concerns has been that the subway must be able to convey its subterranean character.

The project must convey the poetry of the tunnels and submerged spaces to all who walk through the corridors, stairways, or galleries. Attempting to give it another image would be a mistake, thought Foster.

General view of one of the platforms. The upper platform coincides with the space occupied by the tracks, as if the part belonging to the platforms had been raised.

Despite being such a large engineering job, the Bilbao subway is characterised by the painstaking care taken over the details.

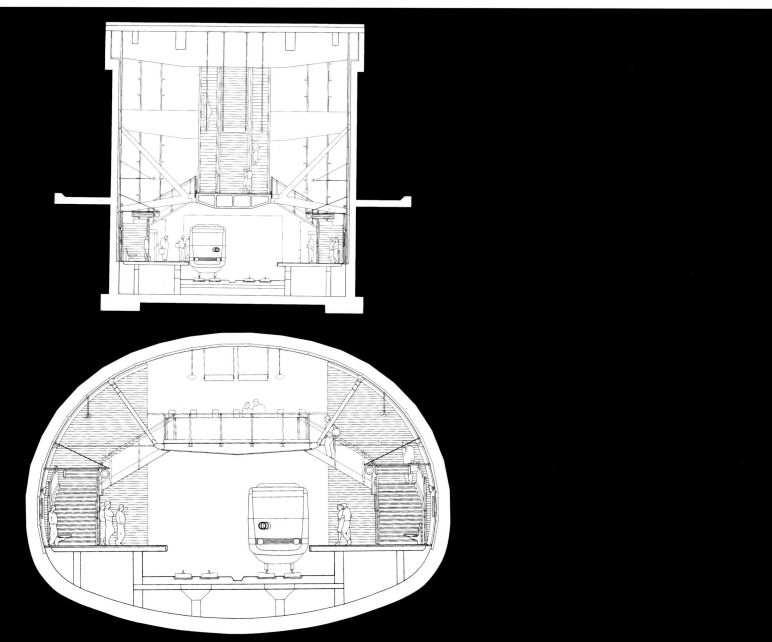

The homogeneity of the finishes conveys an image of simplicity, perfection, and cleanliness. Polished gray concrete and galvanized steel: the interiors are executed almost exclusively with two materials in the same soft, gray tone.

Alameda Bridge and Subway Station

VALENCIA, 1995

Below what had once been the bed of the Turia River lies the Alameda subway station. The riverbed has now been made into the surface of an attractive plaza. This dramatic reconfiguration of the Turia riverbed actually comprises three relatively independent projects—a bridge, a plaza, and a subway station.

As is often the case with Calatrava's projects, the structure of the bridge is itself highly expressive. This inclined arc is at once a structural, figurative, and expressive element of the bridge, and a distinguishing element for the entire project. A single-piece unit spanning 130 meters, the bridge is an arc-shaped, lacquered steel structure.

The structural principles of Calatrava's projects are relatively simple. Even so, each detail is meaningful and each material is chosen taking into consideration its range of technical strengths and limitations. As a result, a bridge by Calatrava is quite capable of becoming a bull, perhaps, or a winged animal poised to take flight.

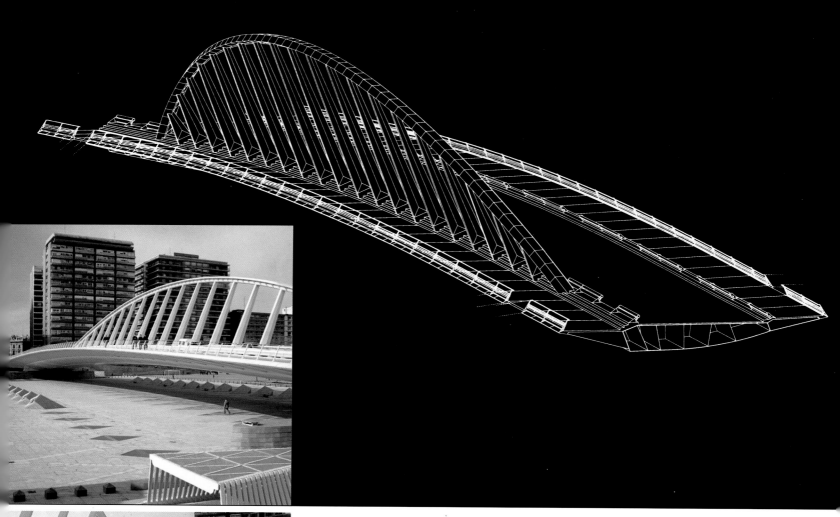

Axonometric drawing of the bridge.

General view.

The structure is made of white, reinforced concrete.

Entrance gate.

Transverse cross-sections.

The subway platform is 63 meters long and 26.6 meters across, with platforms on each side measuring 4 meters, and a central platform measuring 7.5 meters in width. The bridge is interesting in that it is inclined. The 14-meter-high parabolic arc looming above the pedestrian span is inclined 70 degrees away from the horizontal, and is 584 meters long.

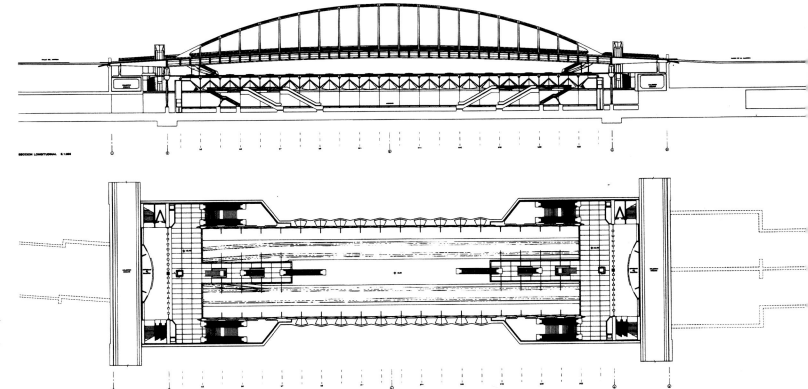

SECCION LONGITUDINAL E.1:200

PLANTA COTA +2.40 E.1:200

Treatment of the subway opening.

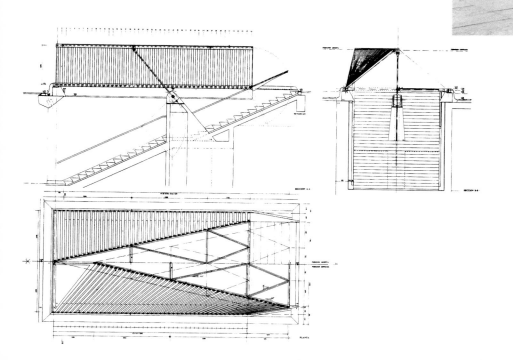

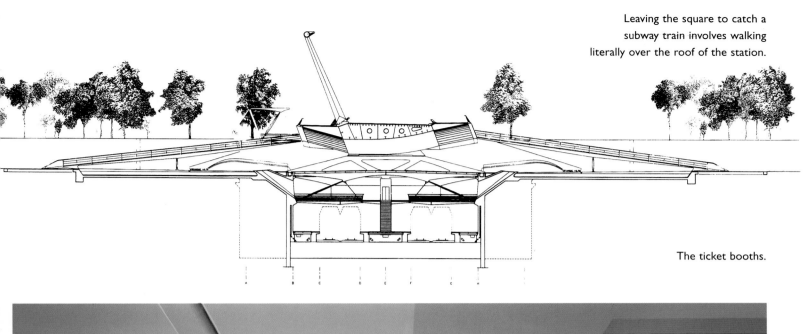

Leaving the square to catch a subway train involves walking literally over the roof of the station.

The ticket booths.

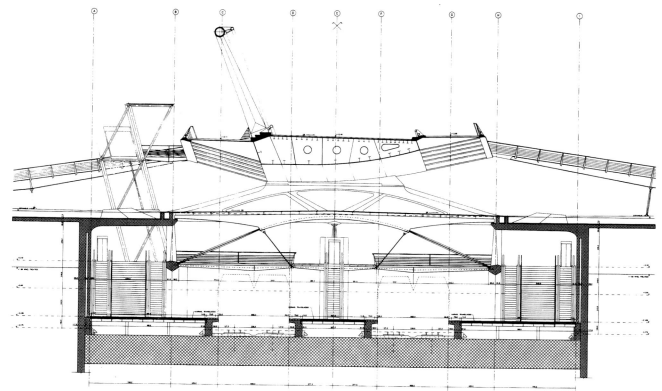

Vénissieux Parilly Subway Station

Lyon, 1993

"The Dead and the Buried: that which is underground, hidden, secret, is always present in the life of a town or city. The water flowing beneath its soil, the galleries threading through its hills, the foundations of its buildings, the crypts under its numerous churches, all this works together to give birth to a parallel world, a world both religious and secular—or perhaps, merely natural."

That paragraph, from a work titled "Dragonflies," is part of what Jourda & Parraudin presented two years prior to beginning their work on the Parilly station. This affirmation of the subterranean as a parallel, sealed, and mysterious world doubtlessly also forms part of their design for this station.

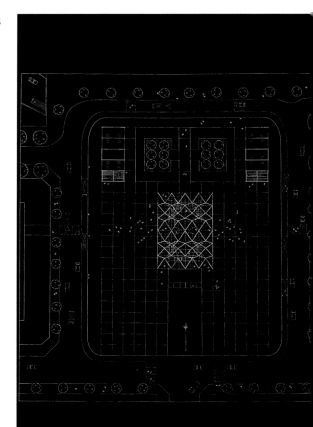

Jourda and Perraudin seem convinced that architecture does not follow the same principles underground as above ground. Strangely, the image created by the canopy covering the station, and the structure of the tunnel itself, appear to be inverses of each other. While the upper suggests the delicate branches of a tree, the lower suggests a cavern, whose stout, inclined pillars are siblings of those found in the crypt of the Colonia Güell by Gaudí. Like Gaudí's pillars, these were also intended to support a building which was never actually constructed.

Detailed view of the façade. The space created by the absence of a planned building is covered with a light, translucent structure with treelike pillars.

Located in a sparsely populated suburb of Lyon at the conjunction of several major highways, the Vénissieux subway is part of an urban plan that also included a building of 10,000 square meters directly above the station. The main lobby of the building was to have served as an access point for the platforms. Because this building was never constructed, the station had to be protected by a temporary roof and enclosure, which ironically now are part of what lends the structure its extraordinary appearance.

View of the vestibule. Although this is an
unfinished project, the fact that pillars
originally intended to bear 300 tons now
support a light, treelike structure gives
the work a sorrowful, elegiac feeling.

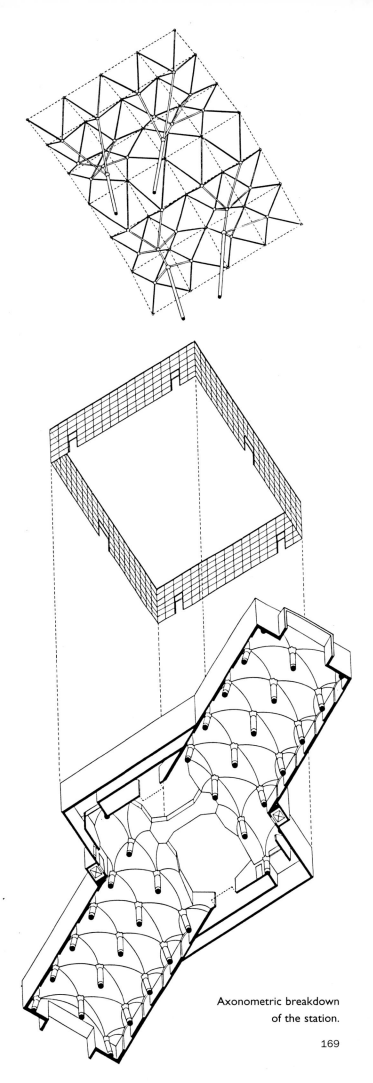

Axonometric breakdown
of the station.

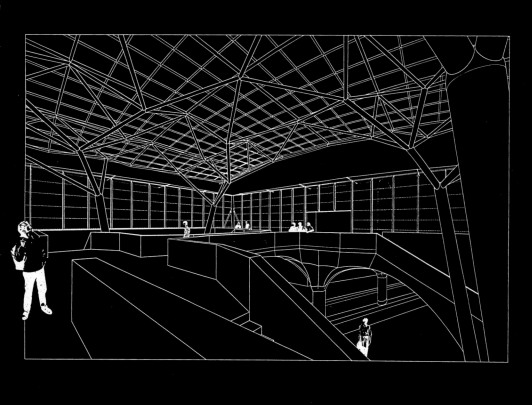

Various views of the
station.

The tilt of the pillars
follows the line of
maximum stress.

Place de l'Homme de Fer

Strasbourg, 1994

Bus and streetcar stops are often an afterthought. On few occasions
do architectural studies examine the impact they will have on the
image of the city. Furthermore, they are often isolated from any
esthetic context and even their locations are chosen haphazardly.
In Strasbourg, the opposite has been true, at least in the case of
one of its city squares.

According to Clapot, the Place de l'Homme de Fer was actually the
result of a hole in the city originally caused by Allied bombing
raids during the Second World War. All around the 70-meter
triangular perimeter of the square the buildings take on varying
scales and styles that jar against each other.

The construction of the new streetcar line was the first stage of an
urban renewal project designed to recover spaces for
pedestrian uses. Recently, the streetcar, along with so-
called "light rail," is recovering some of its former
prestige, as it is now being seen as clean and ecological.

Over 24,000 vehicles pass around the square each day. Two tiles with plaques commemorate a plaza, named Two-Tile Square, which existed at this location for 500 years.

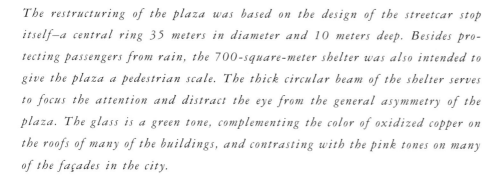

The restructuring of the plaza was based on the design of the streetcar stop itself—a central ring 35 meters in diameter and 10 meters deep. Besides protecting passengers from rain, the 700-square-meter shelter was also intended to give the plaza a pedestrian scale. The thick circular beam of the shelter serves to focus the attention and distract the eye from the general asymmetry of the plaza. The glass is a green tone, complementing the color of oxidized copper on the roofs of many of the buildings, and contrasting with the pink tones on many of the façades in the city.

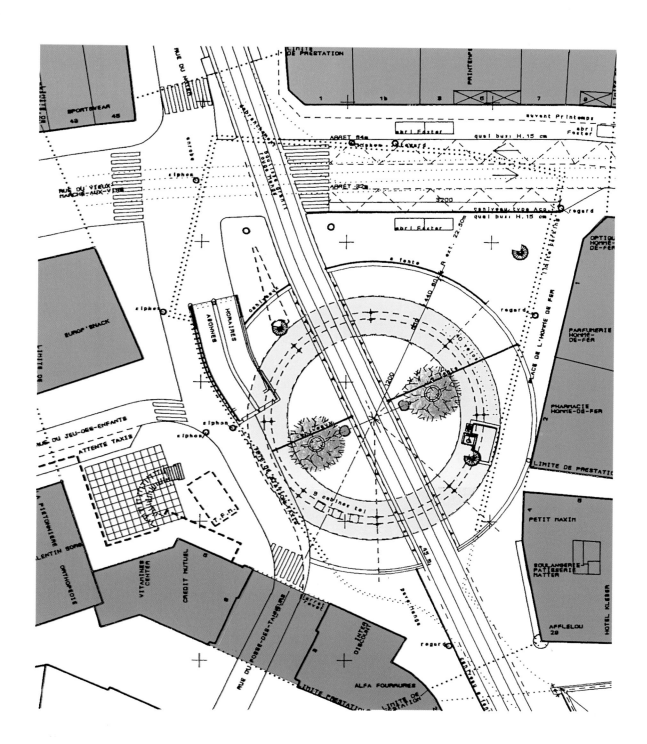

General layout.

The profiles of the perimetral buildings present highly varied, unbalanced depths and heights.

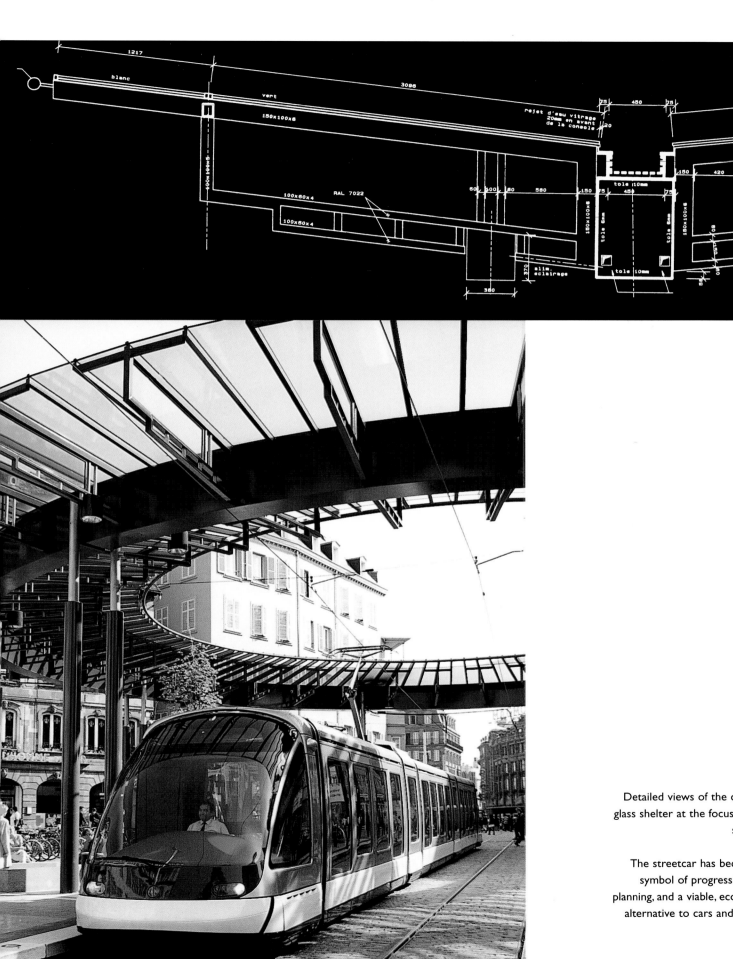

Detailed views of the circular glass shelter at the focus of the square.

The streetcar has become a symbol of progressive city planning, and a viable, ecological alternative to cars and buses.

Bus Stops

HANNOVER, 1994

In spite of the convulsions experienced by art during this past century, the close ties between sculpture and urban design have persisted nearly unchanged. A citizen in the twentieth century lives with works by Henry Moore, Alexander Calder, Claes Oldenburg, Eduardo Chillida, or Richard Serra in the same way that the inhabitants of Rome during the sixteenth century lived with works by Michelangelo or Bernini.

In the past, architecture and sculpture complemented each other and were practically a single discipline. Today, cross-pollination between the two disciplines occurs less than before. Often the sculptor is invited in after a project is nearly completed. In Hannover, however, the current practice of transforming bus stops into sculptures restores the venerable pattern of celebrating architecture and sculpture together.

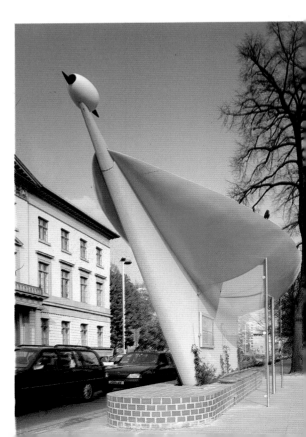

Bus stop on Braunschweiger Platz,
designed by Frank O. Gehry.

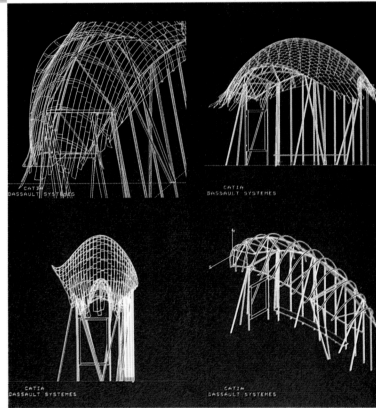

At the architect's request, the siting of the station was moved from a central location to a less dense surrounding, in one of the outskirts of the city that marks out the start of the Alpine route.

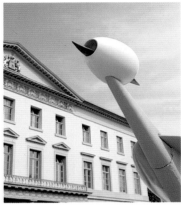

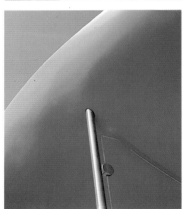

Bus stop designed by
Massimo Iosa Ghini.

This bus stop with a
futuristic appearance is
located in front of a palace in
a classical style, designed in
the last century by G.L.F.
Laves.

The idea for the bus stops project actually began in 1976 with a pavilion at the Venice Biennale. The pavilion, by Joseph Beuys, was titled "Street-Car Stop." Busstops forms part of an ensemble of activities promoted by the Foundation of Lower Saxony called "Art in the Public Sphere," with the aim of promoting contemporary art for public uses. The project director, Lothar Romain, sought architects who were more comfortable approaching architecture as a matter of imagery and who preferred working with shapes to working with spaces. Among the many artists represented is in the project is Ettore Sottsass, founder of the Memphis group and patriarch of the New Design movement.

Streetcar station on Kurt Schumacher Strasse, designed by Alessandro Mendini.

Kurt Schumacher Strasse, in front of the Anzeiger Building, is one of the busiest districts in Hannover. This place was chosen by the Italian artist. The work has received the popular nickname "Dueling Castle."

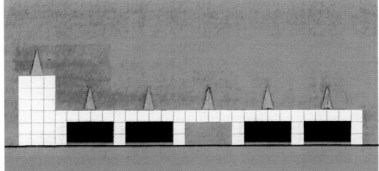

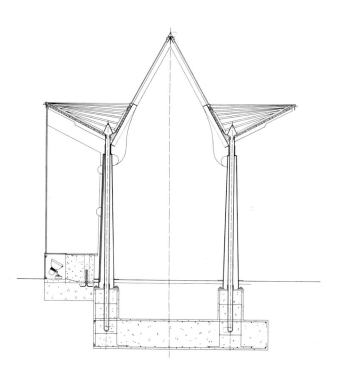

Streetcar station adjoining the city auditorium, on Theodor Heuss Platz, designed by Òscar Tusquets.

For the roof, the Catalan architect used iroko wood in the interior, and copper plate on the exterior. The pillars are stainless steel and the bench is cement, with the seats made of Corian acrylic resin.

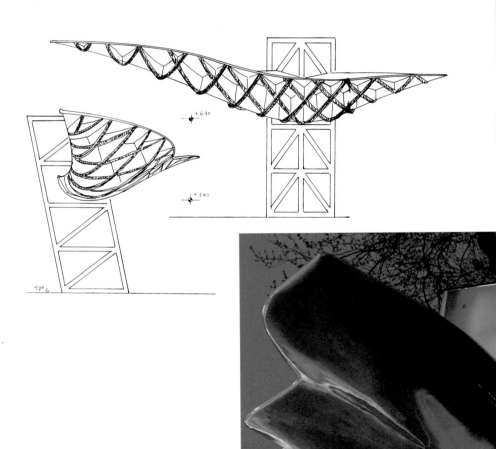

Station next to the
Sprengel Museum, designed
by Heike Mülhaus.

An architectonic work of these
reduced dimensions allows direct
translation of the idea into reality.

BUS STOP

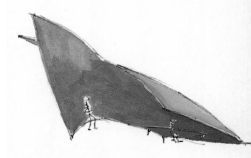

PAUL ANDREU

1938 Bordeaux-Caudéran (France).
1958 Graduation from the Polytechnic School.
1963 Bridges and Roads Engineering Qualification.
1967-1974 Charles de Gaulle Airport, Paris.
1970-1990 Roissy railway station. Cruas nuclear Central. Grand Arc de La Défense (together with J.O. Spreckelsen), and the airports of Abu Dhabi (United Arab Emirates), Dacca (Bangladesh), Djarkata (Indonesia), Dar Es-Salaam (Tanzania), Terminal II of El Cairo Montpelier, Terminal II of Nice, Terminal II Charles de Gaulle, Brunei, Conakry (Guinea).
1990-97 Jump Trampoline for the 1992 Winter Games. Extension to the Orly airport. Terminal of the Channel Tunnel. Interchange Module for the CDG airport. Airports of Sanya (China), Bordeaux, Guadalupe and Eldoret (Kenya).
1995 Aga Khan Prize.

JAUME BACH

1943 Sabadell (Spain).
1970 Qualified as Architect.

GABRIEL MORA

1941 Barcelona (Spain).
1966 Qualified as Architect.

BACH/MORA

1980-90 Stations at Bellaterra and Can Ros. Remodelling of the squares in Gracia. The Jujol, Mercè Rosell and Torre Balldovina schools. Perill Multi-sports hall. Cavas Raventós.
1990-97 Field Hockey Olympic Stadium, Tarrassa. Olympic Village Telephone Exchange, Barcelona. Sabadell station. 90 homes in Torreguitart. Operations Centre of the Rubí Railway. Casa Salgado. School in Mollet.

JAN BENTHEM

1952 Amsterdam (Holland).
1978 Qualified as Architect at the Technical University of Delft.

MELS CROUWEL

1953 Amsterdam (Holland).
1978 Qualified as Architect at the Technical University of Delft.

BENTHEM CROUWEL

1980-1990 Viviendas en Oldenzaal, Hazeldonk, Gennep, Nieuweschans, Ter Apel, Venlo.
1990-1997 Museo De Pont, Tilburg. Offices Wagonlit and Hotel Ibis, Amsterdam. Nieuw Land Poldermuseum, Lelystad. Torre Malie, Den Haag.

SANTIAGO CALATRAVA

1951 Benimamet (Spain).
1974 Qualified as Architect.
1979-81 Title and Doctorate of Structures at E.T.H. Zurich.
1982-1990 Ernsting factory, Coesfeld (Germany). School in Wohlen (Switzerland). Tabourettli Cabaret, Basle. Railway stations in Zurich and Lucerne. Bridges in Barcelona, Créteil, Valencia and Mérida.
1990-1997 Place du L'Heritage, Toronto. Telecommunications Tower in Barcelona. Lyon-Satôlas TGV station. Kuwait EXPO'92 pavilion. Bilbao airport. Remodelling of the St. John the Divine Cathedral, New York. Bridges in Seville, Ripoll and Valencia.

GUY CLAPOT

1955 Dakar (Senegal).
Studios in Lyon and Strasbourg.
1981 Own studio.
1985-1990 Prehistorical Museum, Solutré. School of Architecture of Strasbourg.
1990-1997 University Library of the Faculty of Letters, Mulhouse. Popular National Theatre, Villeurbanne. Remodelling of the sector of the Kléber Square, Strasbourg.

CURTIS WORTH FENTRESS, AIA, RIBA

1947 Greensboro, North Carolina (USA).
1972 Qualified as Architect. University of North Carolina State.
1972-1977 Collaborating architect for I.M. Pei and Partners (NY).
1977-1980 Architect with the company, Kohn Pedersen Fox (NY).
1980 Founded C.W. Fentress and Associates (after 1990, C.W. Fentress, J.H. Bradburn Associates), in Colorado. Main projects: Colorado Convention Centre, 1999 Broadway, One DTC, Jefferson County Government Centre.

SIR NORMAN FOSTER

1935 Manchester (United Kingdom).
1961 Qualified as Architect.
1967 Founded, in conjunction with Wendy Foster, Foster Associates.
1968-1983 Collaborated on several projects with Buckminster Fuller.
1967-1990 Offices of the Hong Kong and Shanghai Bank in Hong Kong.
1990 Founded Sir Norman Foster and Partners.
1990-1997 Stansted airport. Century Tower, Tokyo. Carré d'Arts, Nîmes. Library at the University of Cranfield. Law Faculty of Cambridge. Joselyn Art museum, Nebraska. Commerzbank offices, Frankfurt.

FRANK O. GEHRY

1930 Toronto (Canada).
Studied at the University of South California and Harvard.
1962 Founded Frank O. Gehry and Associates, Inc.
1979 Pritzer Prize.
1970-1990 Ron Davies Studio, Malibu. Concord Pavilion, Concord. Gehry House, Santa Monica. Aerospace Museum of California, Los Angeles. Winton House Guest Pavilion. Vitra Museum, Wheil am Rhein.
1990-1997 Guggenheim Museum, Bilbao. Eurodisney, Paris. Iowa Advanced Technology Laboratories.

MASSIMO IOSA GHINI

1959 Borgo Tossignano (Italy).
1982-1990 Jobs as an illustrator on several magazines. Collaborated with RAI, the Italian television. Furnishing for MEMPHIS. Own collection *Dynamic* (Roscoe Prize, USA). Won the competition for the square in front of the Pompidou Centre. Exhibitions in Los Angeles, New York, Vienna, Paris, Singapore,...
1990-1997 Working with an automobile company and another making glasses. Workshop in the Vitra Museum. Individual exhibition in Munich. *European House* programme.

ARNE HENRIKSEN

1144 Sondre Land (Norway).
1963-1965 Ecole Nationale des travaux Publics, Paris.
1966-1971 Norges Tekniske Hogskole (Architecture department).
1975-1989 Chief Architect of the architectural division of the Norwegian railways.
1989 Founded his own architect's office.
1989-1992 Professor at the School of Architecture of Oslo.

Main projects: Moelven Station. Building for turning wheels in Lodalen. Holmlia station. Maintenance hall in Lodalen. Stations at Slependen and Sandvika.

HELMUT JAHN, FAIA

1940 Nuremberg (Germany).
1965 Graduated from the Technische Hochschule of Munich.
1967 Graduated from the Illinois Institute of Technology.
1967 Entered C.F. Murphy Associates.
1982 President of Murphy/Jahn.
1985-1990 362 West Street, Durban. North Western Atrium Centre, Chicago. Park Avenue Tower, New York. O'Hare airport.
1990-1997 Livingston Plaza, New York. Two Liberty Place, Philadelphia. 120n, LaSalle Street, Chicago. One America Plaza, San Diego. Roissy Hyatt Regency, Paris. Munich Order Centre. Hitachi Tower, Singapore. Caltex House, Singapore. Hotel Kempinski, Munich. Ku-Damm, Berlin. Pallas, Stuttgart.

FRANÇOISE-HÉLÈNE JOURDA

1955 Lyon (France).
1979 Qualified as Architect.

GILLES PERRAUDIN

1949 Lyon (France).
1977 Qualified as Architect.

JOURDA & PERRAUDIN

1985-1990 Lanterne School, Cergy-Pontoise. Lyon School of Architecture. Memorial to the Deportation in Lyon. Experimental houses in Stuttgart. Houses Tassin-la-Demi-Lune. Houses and offices Zac Didot, Paris. International Scholar Town, Lyon.
1990-1997 Student's residence in Ecully. University of Marne la Vallée. Social housing Lyon 4°. Parilly station. Academy of the Ministry for the Interior in Herne Sodingen, Germany. Melun Palace of Justice.

ALESSANDRO MENDINI

1931 Milan (Italy).
Editor of Casabella, Modo and Domus. Industrial and furniture designer.
1968 Started an Association with his brother Francesco and formed the **Atelier Mendini**.
1968-1990 Offices, houses and commercial malls in Taranto. Discotheque in Crema. Alessi House. Tower in Gibellina. Theatre in Arezzo.
1990-1997 Groningen museum. Merone museum.

HEIKE MÜLHAUS

1954 Wiesbaden-Sonnenburg (Germany).
1981 Design and ceramics studies. Founded the *Cocktail* project.
Designs for Blaupunkt, Mira-X, Belus, AG, Wohlen/Schweiz, Alessi, Braunschweig. Exhibitions in Germany, Italy, USA, France.
1992-1997 Manager and designer for the *Cocktail* company.

ROB WELLINGTON QUIGLEY FAIA

1969 Architecture studies. University of Utah.
1969-1971 Served in the Peace Corps in Chile as a designer of low-cost housing.
1973-1990 Multiple detached residences in San Diego, La Jolla, Del Mar, Palos Verdes, Coronado, Escondido,... Linda Vista library, San Diego. Escondido Transit Centre.
1990-1997 Island Inn 202 Private room hotel. Oliver Stone's house. Glass house on Capistrano beach. Esperanza Gardens Apartments. UCSD Educational Centre, La Joya. Houses in Camino Real. Hotel Alma Place, Palo Alto. Episcopal church of San David, San Diego. Alden Residency, Beverly Hills. Lasting Residency, Poway.

DENIS SLOAN

1934 Tahiti (Polynesia).
1939-1953 Adolescence in Morocco.
1949 Qualified as Airline Pilot (the youngest in Morocco).
1955-1996 Qualified as Architect at the Paris l'Ecole de Beaux-Arts.
1958-1968 Worked in the studio of Paul Herbé and Jean Le Couteur.
1969 Own studio.
1970-1990 French Pavilion at the EXPO'72 in Osaka.. 2nd prize in the competition for La Villette. Technology University of N'Gaundéré (Cameroon). THOMSON Research Centre at Saint-Egrève. Construction of the new town of Salahaldeen (Iraq). Telecommunications centre at Sofia-Antipolis.
1990-1997 Zenith Theatre in Nancy. Dôme Hall in Marseilles.

ETTORE SOTTSASS

1917 Innsbruck (Austria).
1939 Qualified at the Polytechnic University of Turin.
1942 Founded own design studio in Milan.
From **1958** Chief design consultant at Olivetti.
1975 Founded Sottsass Associati.
1981 Founded MEMPHIS reference of the *New Design*. His jobs as an industrial and furniture designer cover one of the most widely acknowledged works in the worldwide panorama.

OSCAR TUSQUETS

1941 Barcelona (Spain).
1960 School of Arts and Crafts.
1965 Qualified as Architect.
1964 Founded the PER studio (with Cirici, Bonet and Clotet).
1987 Founded Díaz & Assoc. with Carlos Díaz Tusquets.
1968-1990 Regás House. House on the Isle of Pantelleria. Mae-West hall in the Dalí museum in Figueres (together with Dalía and Mireia Riera). La Balsa restaurant. Palau de la Música of Barcelona.
1990-1997 Restaurants in the Parc de la Villette. Cavas Chandon. Houses in Fukuoka and the Olympic Village in Barcelona.

GASTON VALENTE

1951 Thionville (France).
1977 Qualified as Architect at the Strasbourg School of Architecture.
1981 Inaugurated his own office in Strasbourg.
1984 Schoenau Club House.
1988-1997 Houses in Ostwald; Epernay, Lautebourg, Tethel and Strasbourg. Leisure Centre in Florange. Burrough centre in Ostwald. Sarre-union offices. Museum in Le Hohwald.

MEINHARD VON GERKAN

1935 Riga. (Letonia).
1939 Moved to Poland.
1942 Father died in the war.
1945 His mother dies and he moves to Germany.
1964 Qualified as Architect in Berlin.
1965 Becomes an associate at Volkwin Marg.
1965-1990 Max-Planck Institute, Lindau. Sports Centre, Luxembourg. Berlin-Tegel airport. ARAL AG, Bochum. Psychiatric wing, Ricling. BAU 78 housing, Hamburg. Ministry of the Interior, Kiel. Schools at Bad, Hamburg, Braunschweig.
1990-1997 Own house and office, Hamburg. Cultural centres in Bielefeld and Lübeck. Airports in Stuttgart and Hamburg. Offices, factories and commercial centres: Deutsche Revision AG, Frankfurt. Miro Datensysteme, Braunschweig. Lufthansa, Hamburg. Duisburg Gallery.